Hey there! Let's have fun drawing a cute panda together! I'll show you step by step how to do it. First, we'll start with a simple circle. That's going to be the panda's head.

Next, let's draw two smaller circles inside the big circle for the panda's eyes. They should be a little towards the top and close together.

Now, let's add a small oval-shaped nose right below the eyes. And for the mouth, draw a little curve right under the nose.

Great! Now it's time to give our panda some ears. Draw two small half circles on either side of the head. They should be like little curved triangles.

Almost done! Let's add some details. Draw two small circles inside the eyes for pupils. And don't forget to add some lines on the ears to make them look furry.

Lastly, let's draw the panda's body. It's like a big oval shape connected to the bottom of the head. And you can add some lines on the body to show the panda's fur.

And there you go! You've drawn a cute panda! Wasn't that fun? Practice drawing more pandas, and soon you'll be a panda drawing expert! Keep up the great work!

Panda Drawing Book for Kids

Of course! Let's focus on below pictures of the 9 steps to draw a panda. We'll take it one step at a time when we learn how to draw the panda in more detail on the upcoming pages.

Each step will help us understand how to draw the panda better.

We'll start with simple shapes like circles and ovals for the head, ears, and body. Then, we'll add more details like the eyes, nose, mouth, and furry lines on the ears. Finally, we'll complete our panda drawing with some finishing touches to make it look adorable!

Get ready to learn and have fun drawing pandas step by step!

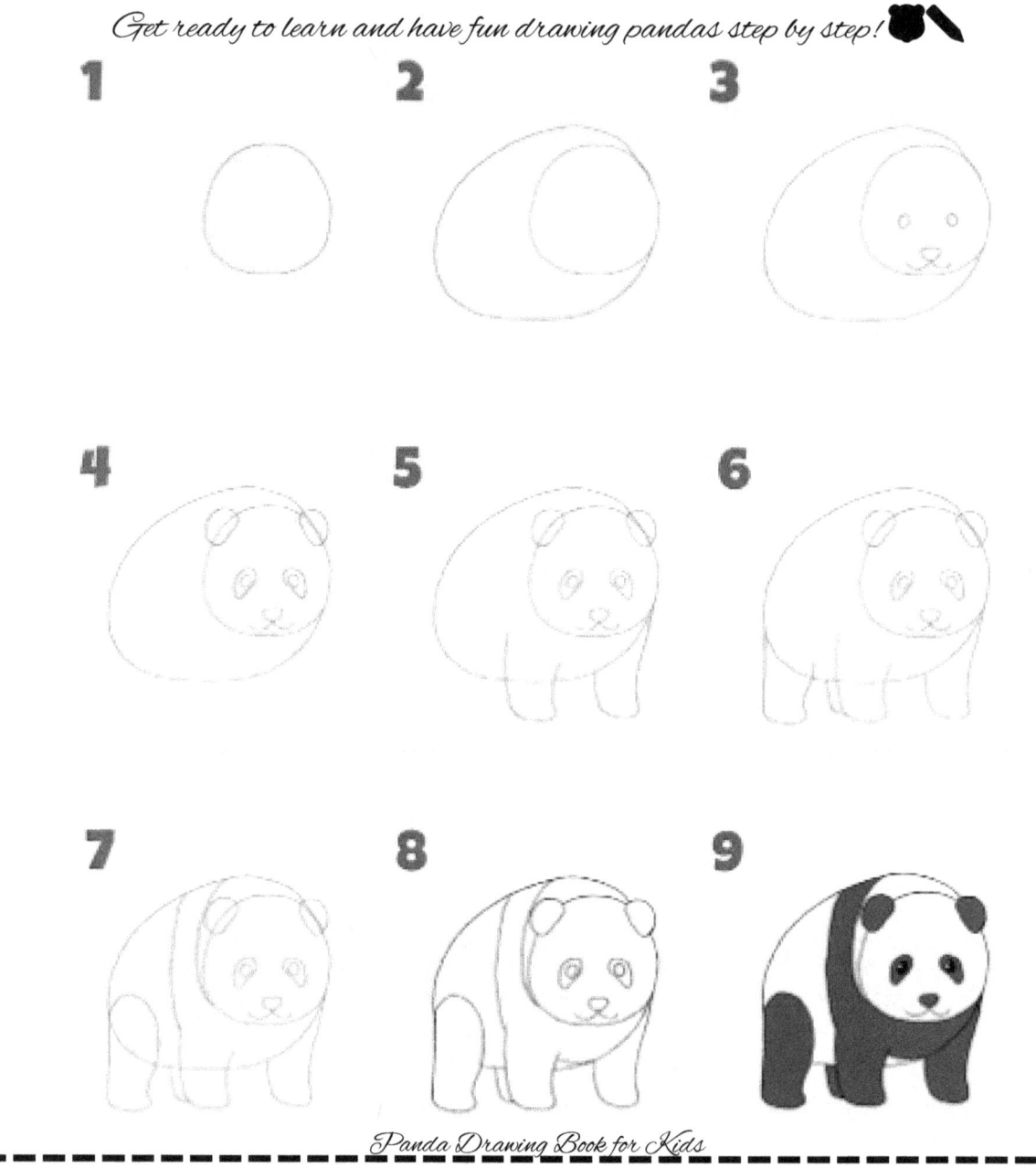

Panda Drawing Book for Kids

Step 1: Draw the outline of the head. Begin by drawing an oval-shaped figure. This oval will serve as the basic shape for the panda's head.

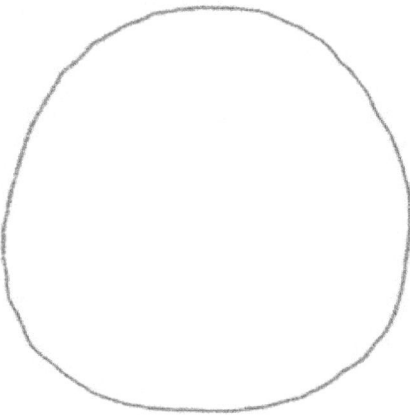

Step 2: Draw the outline of the panda's torso. Sketch a long, curved line near the previously drawn outline of the head. This line will represent the body of the panda, connecting to the head.

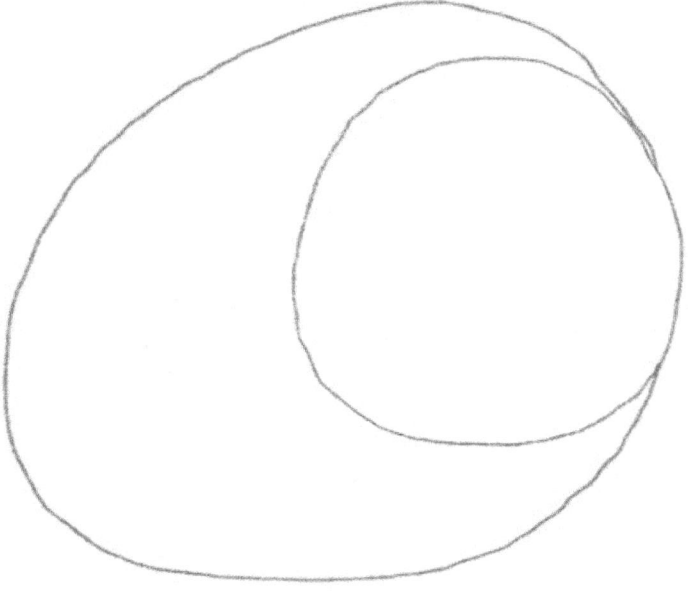

Panda Drawing Book for Kids

Step 3: To add facial features, draw two identical ovals for the panda's eyes. Then, draw two arcs for the eyebrows and a curved line below for the mouth. These details bring life to the panda's face.

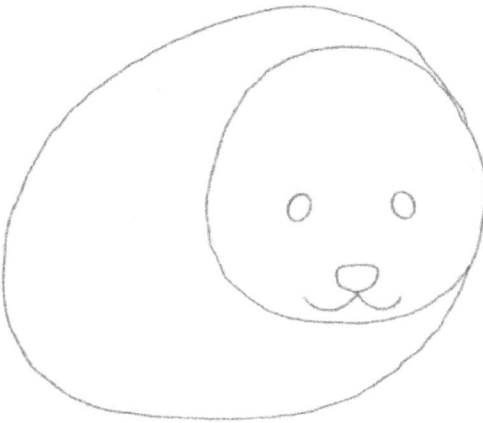

Step 4: To sketch the ears, draw two symmetrical shapes on top of the panda's head. Then, add two curved lines around the eyes. These lines will form the spots around the panda's eyes.

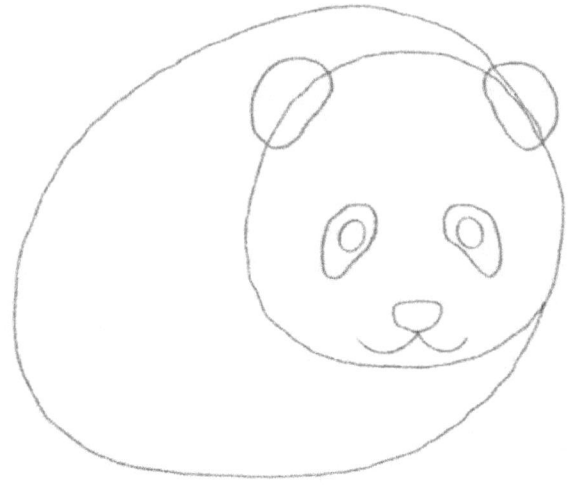

Step 5: To depict the front legs, draw two curved lines in front of the panda's torso, curving gently downward. These lines represent the panda's front legs.

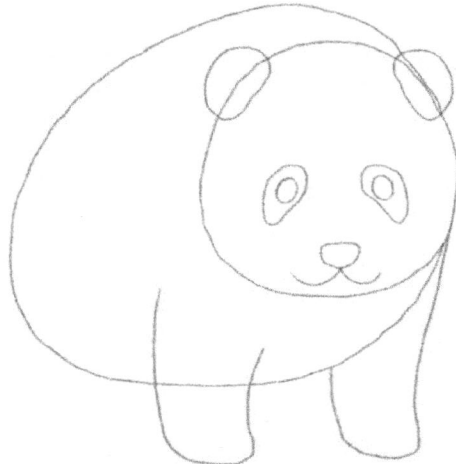

Step 6: To show the hind legs, draw two curved lines at the back of the torso. One should be longer and slightly curved, the other shorter. These lines depict the panda's hind legs.

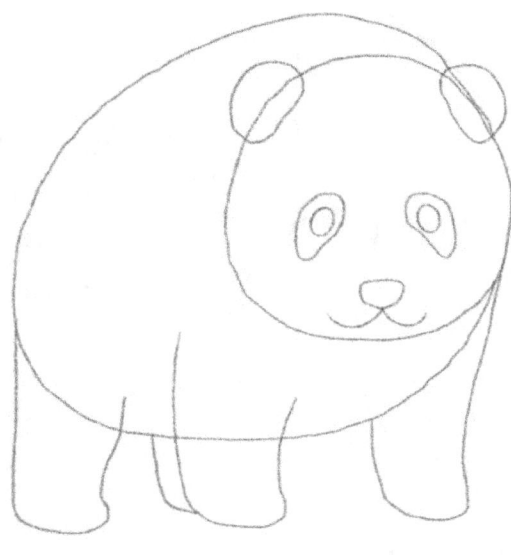

Step 7: Add details. Connect the edges of the previously drawn line to complete the outline of the panda's body. Additionally, draw two curved lines on the back to add texture and detail to the panda's fur.

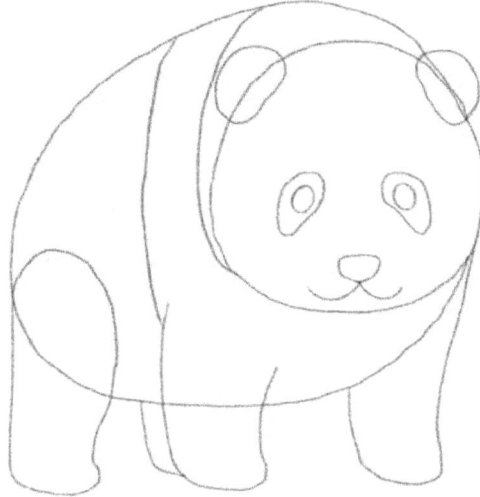

Step 8: Correct inaccuracies. Use the eraser to remove any auxiliary lines, leaving behind only the final outline of the panda. This step helps clean up the drawing and make it look polished.

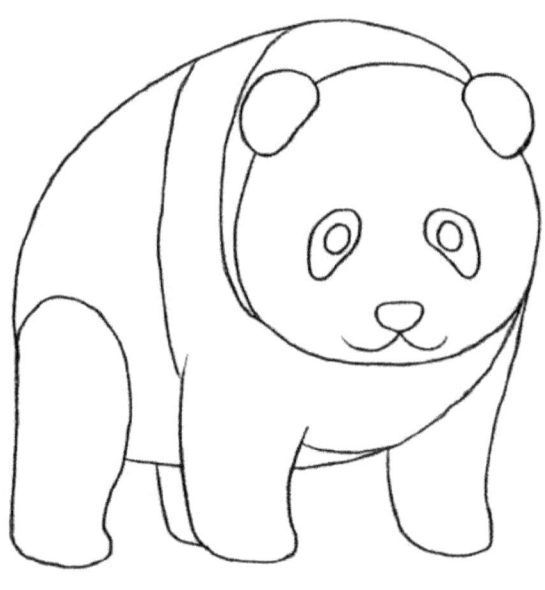

Step 9: Color the drawing. Use gray and black colors to fill in the panda bear's body, leaving the areas around the eyes white. Add highlights to the eyes to make them sparkle and bring the panda to life.

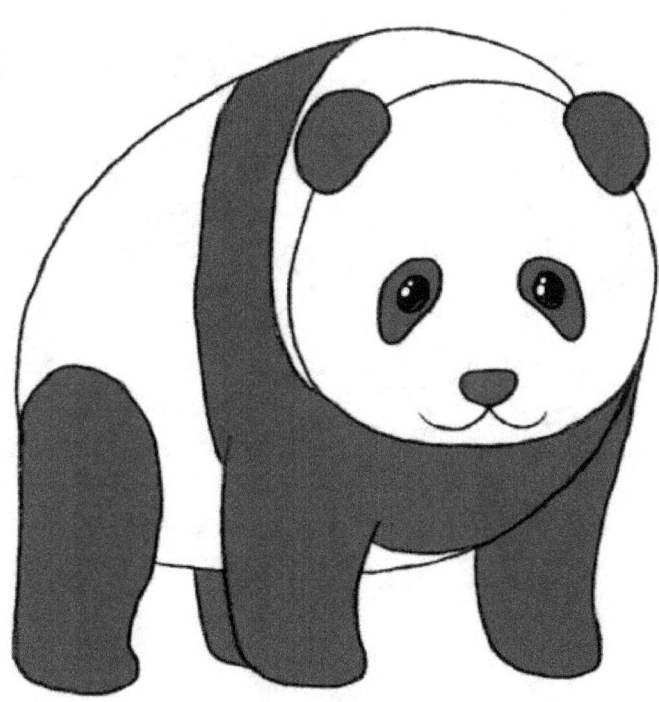

The panda, known for its iconic black and white fur, symbolizes peace and conservation. Endangered due to habitat loss and poaching, efforts are underway to protect these gentle giants. Their bamboo diet and playful demeanor inspire conservation, their colors embodying hope amid challenges.

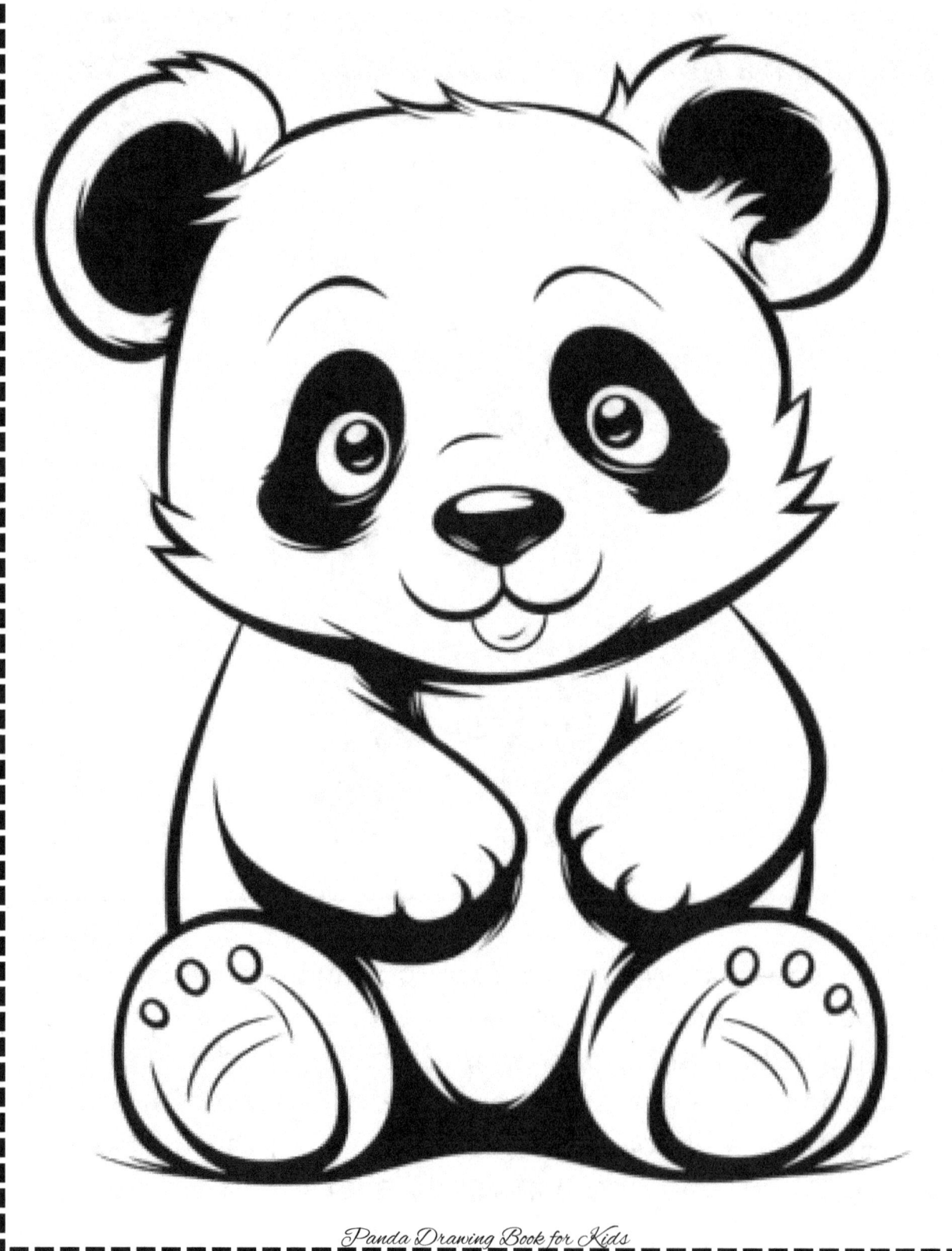

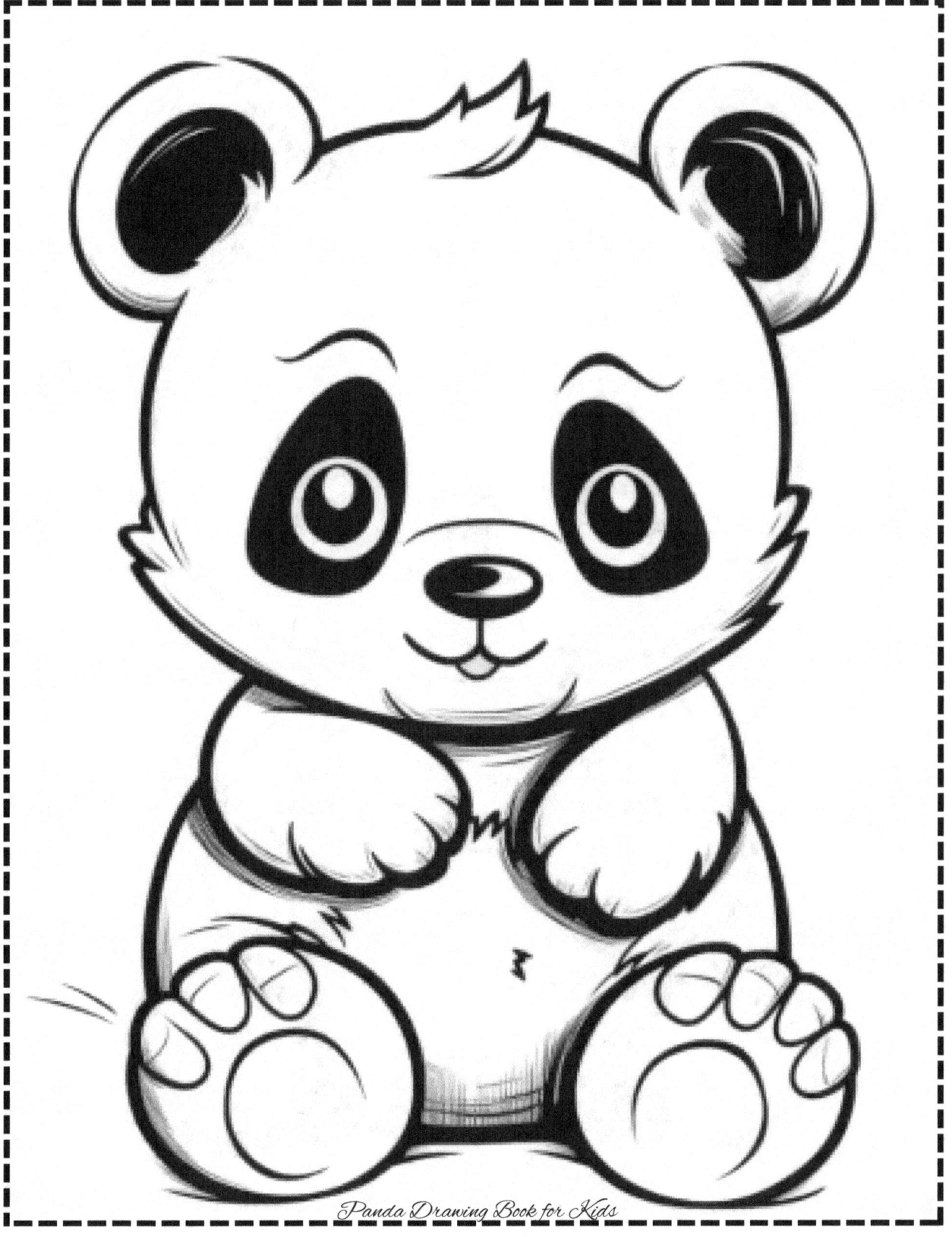

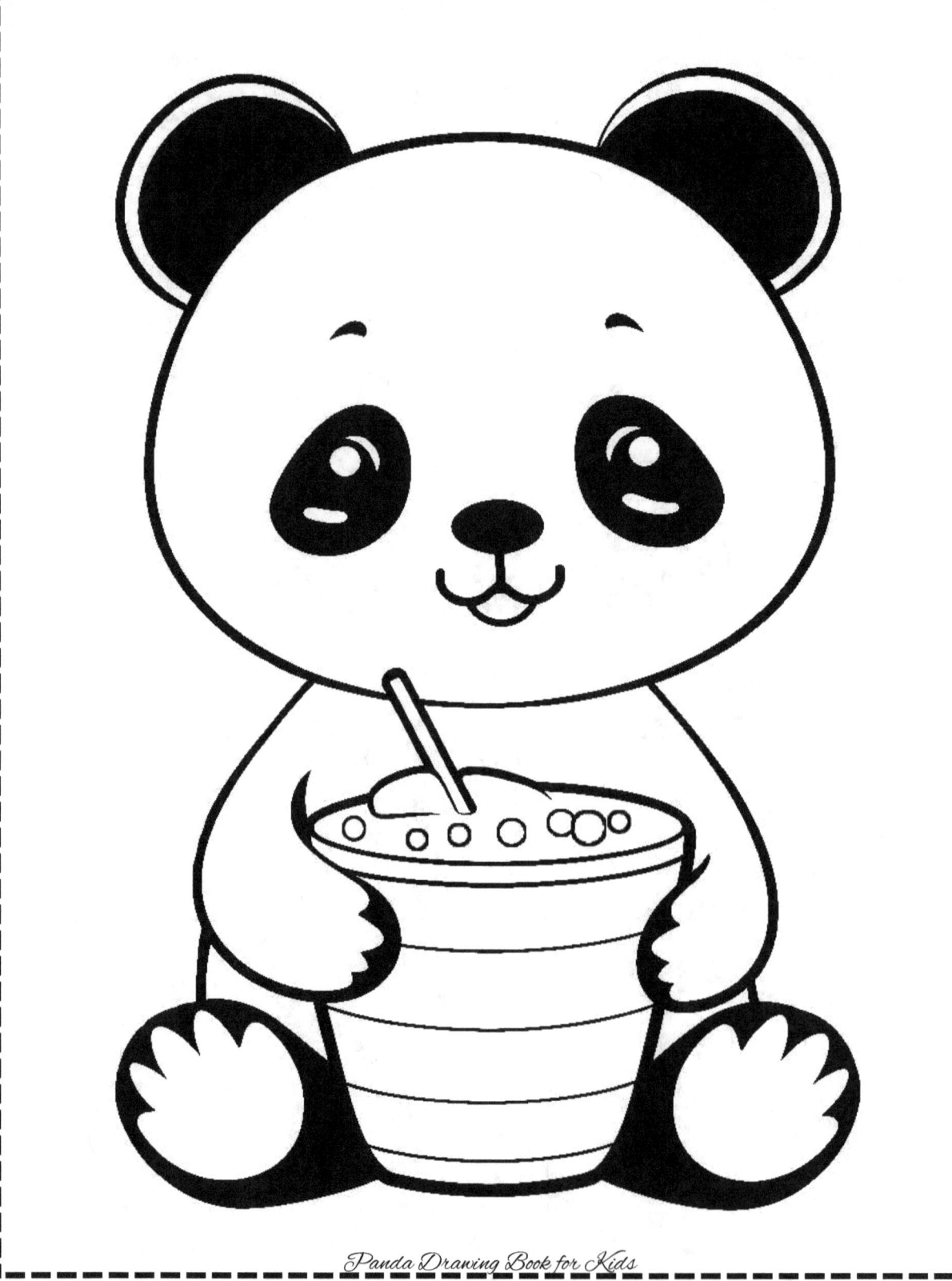

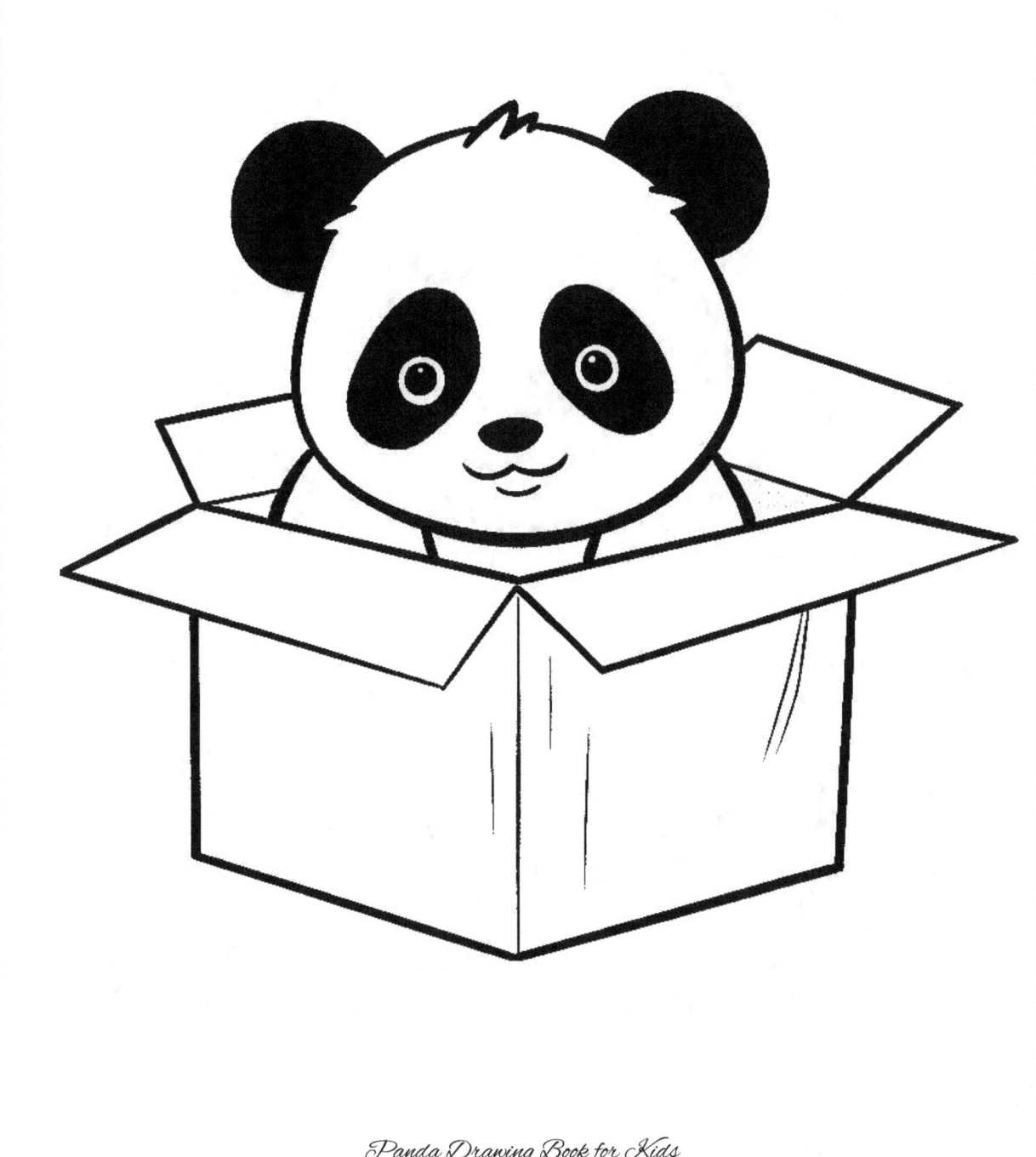

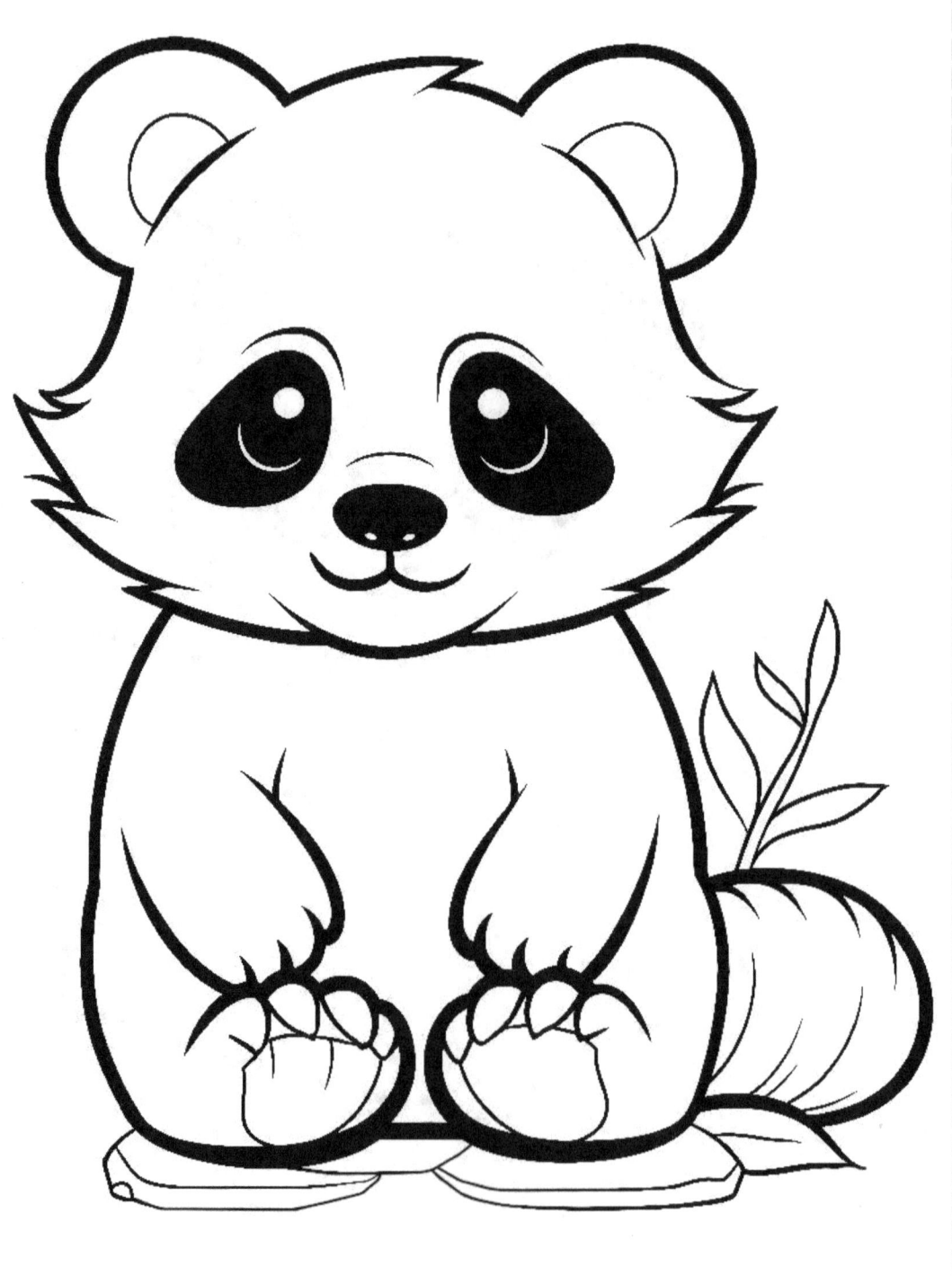

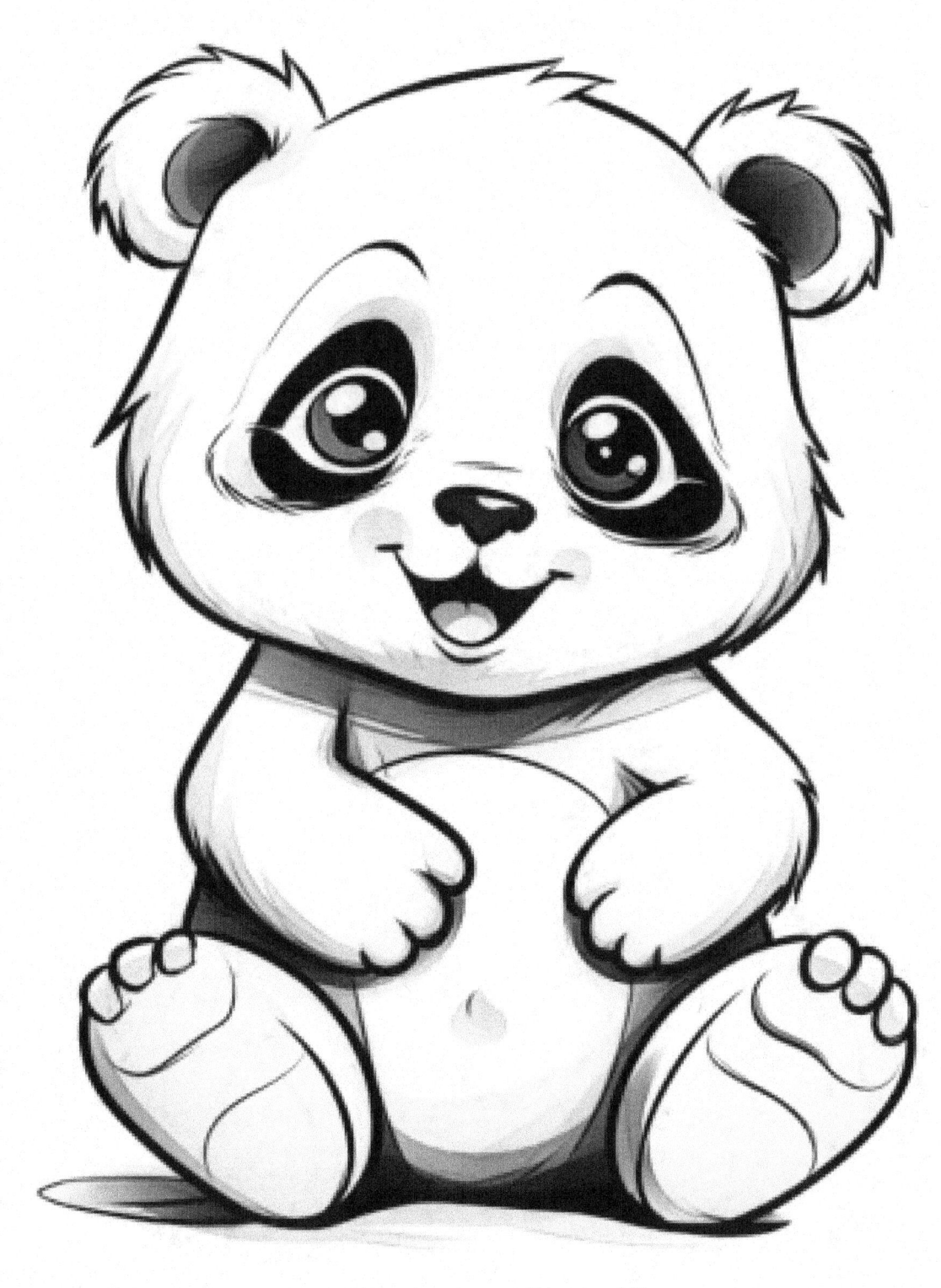

Panda Drawing Book for Kids

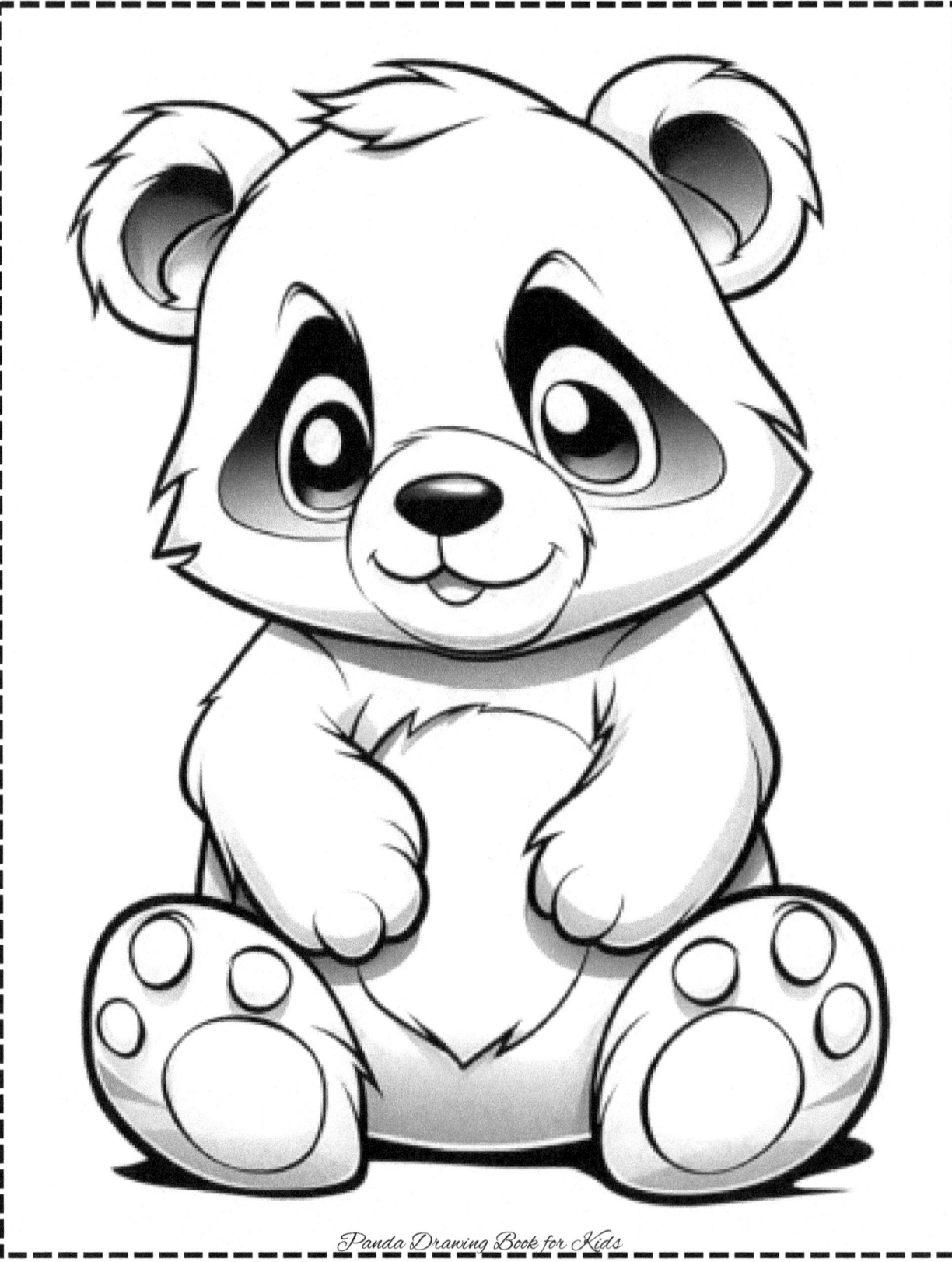

Panda Drawing Book for Kids

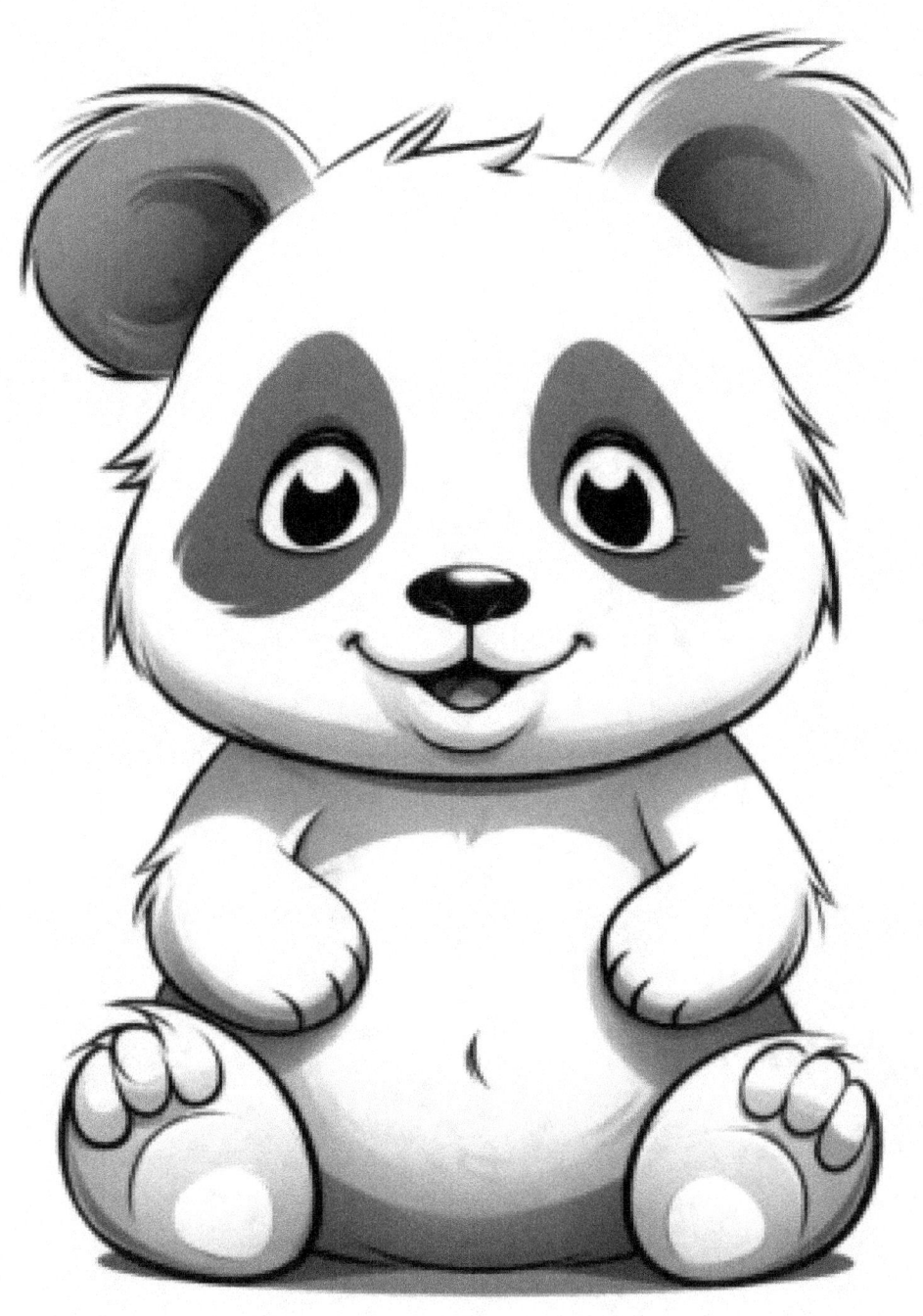

Panda Drawing Book for Kids

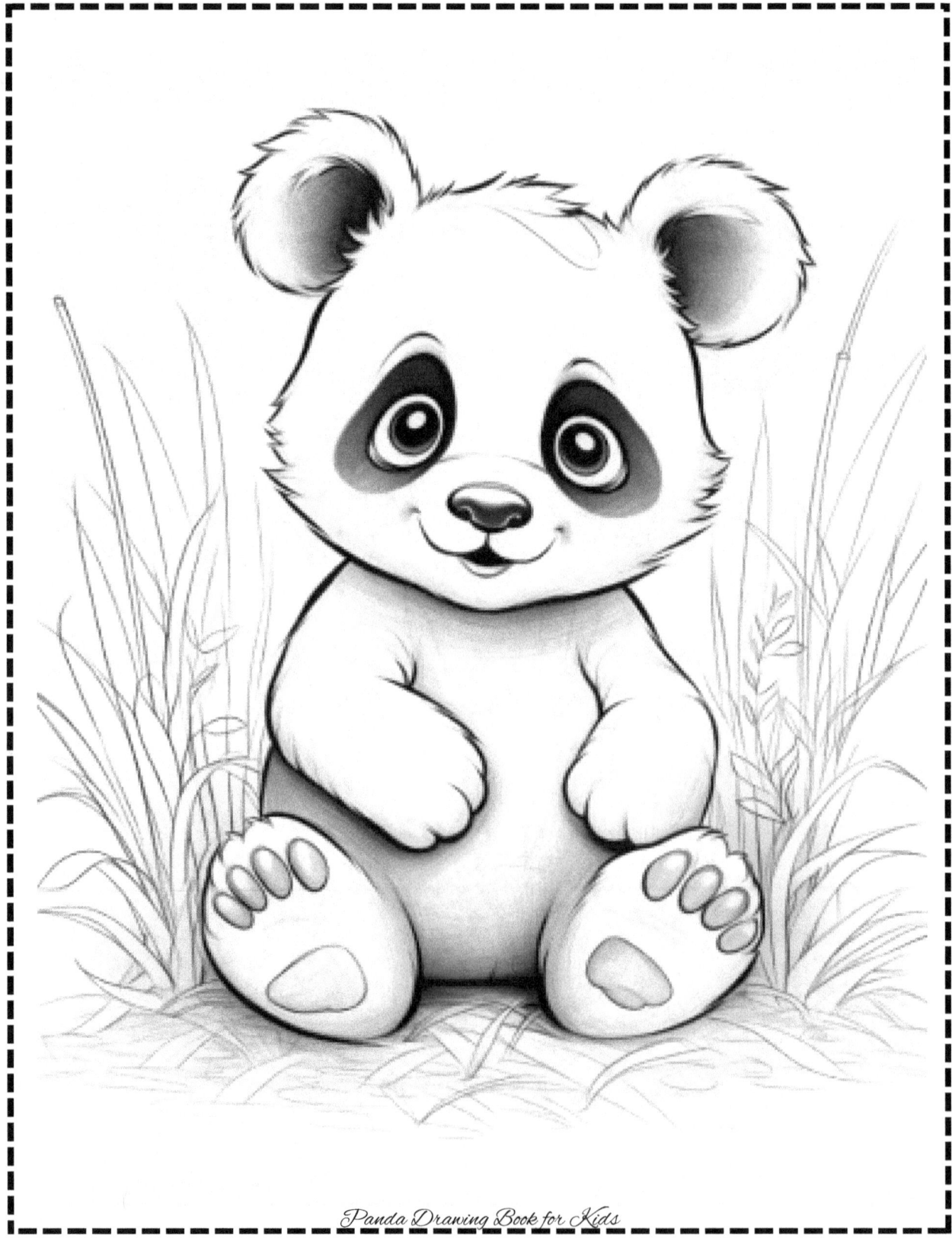

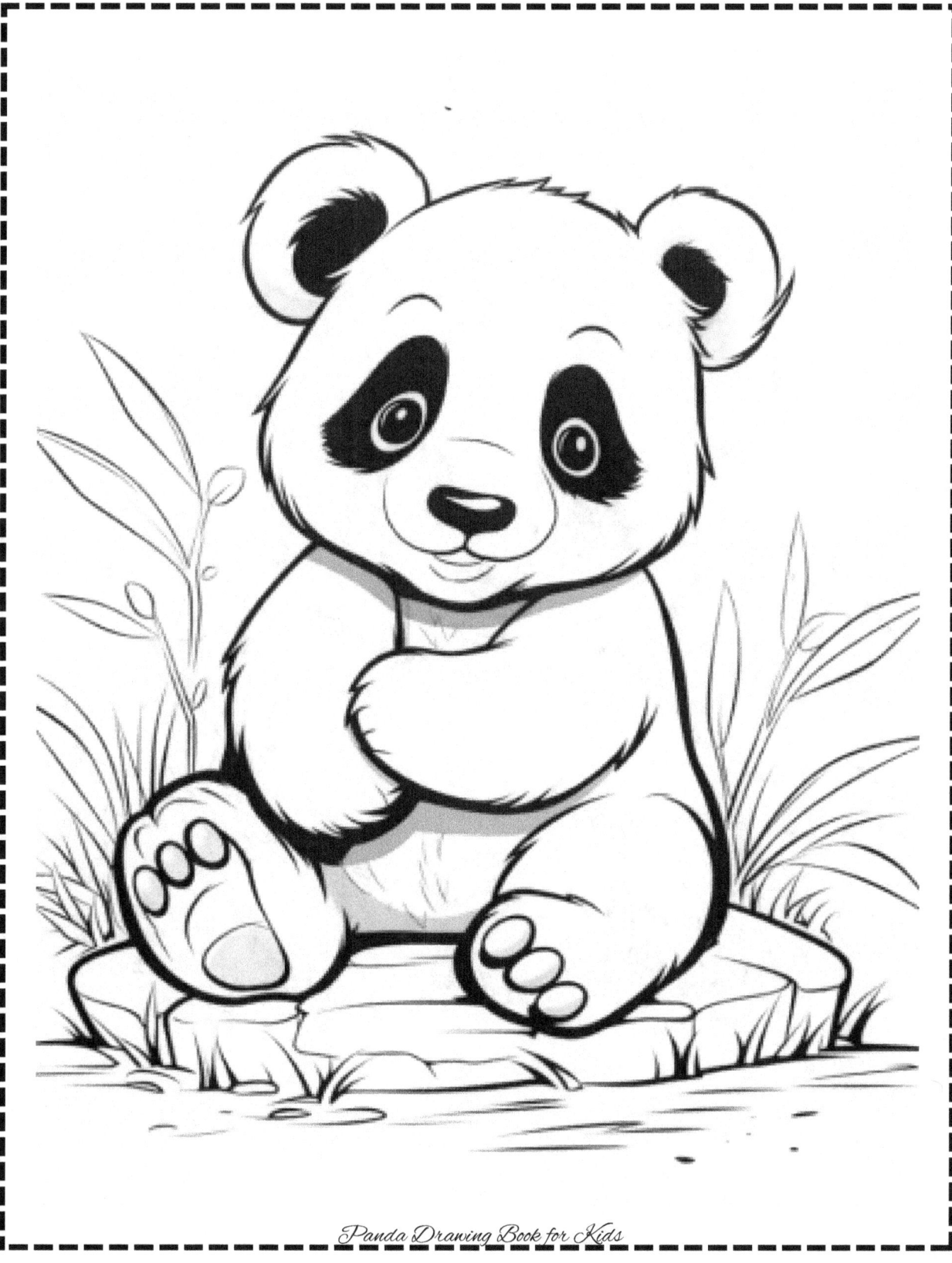

Panda Drawing Book for Kids

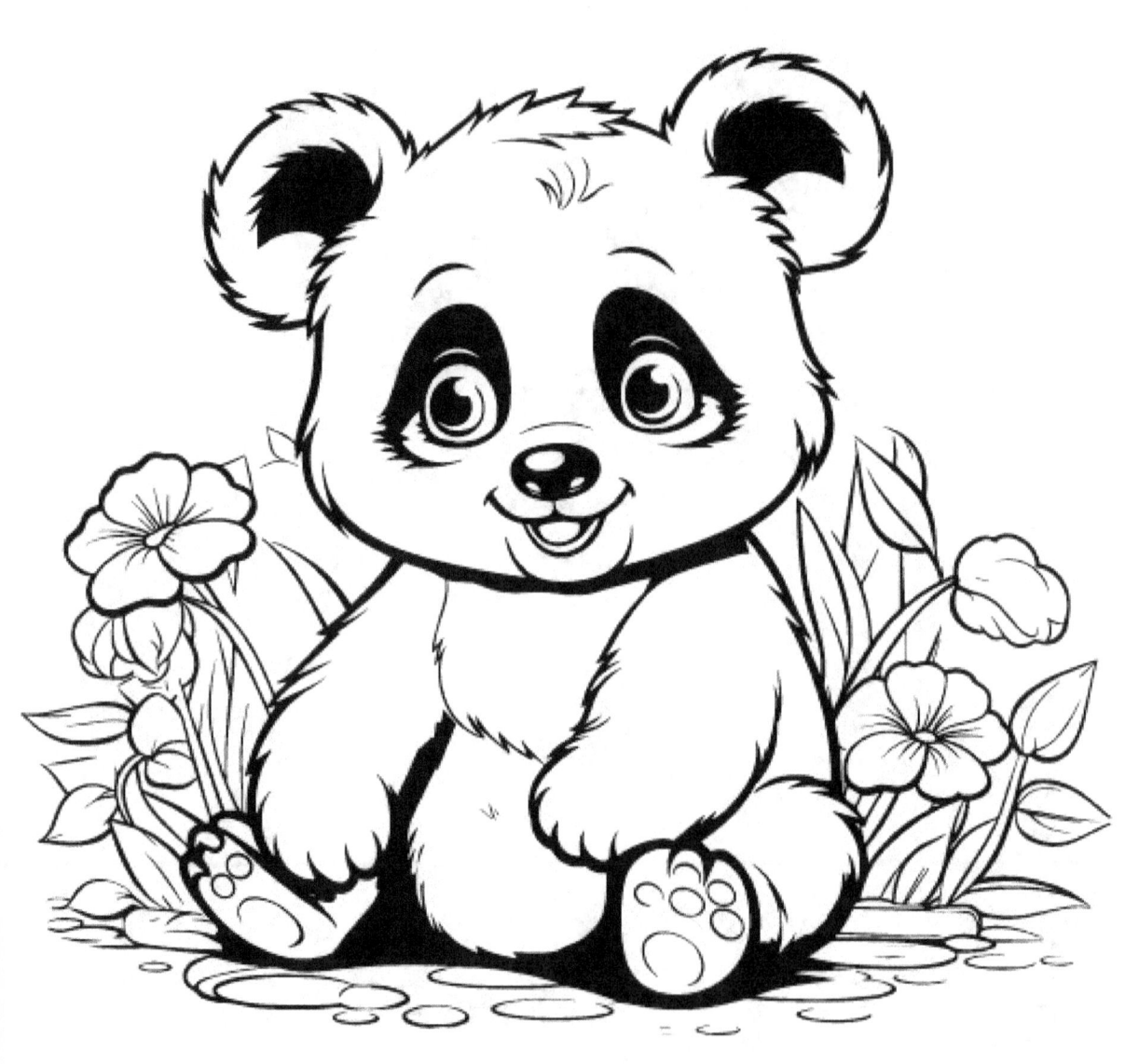

Panda Drawing Book for Kids

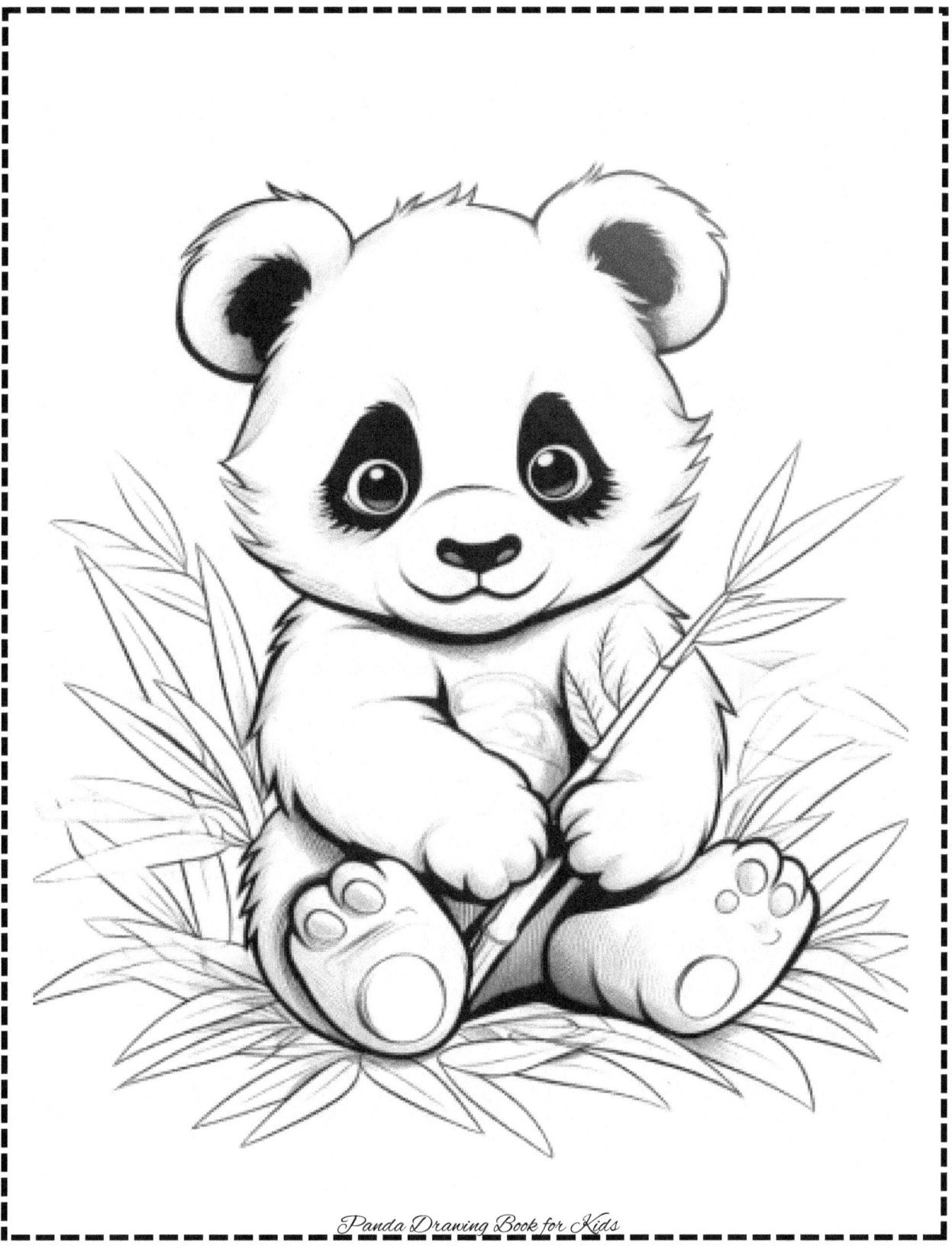

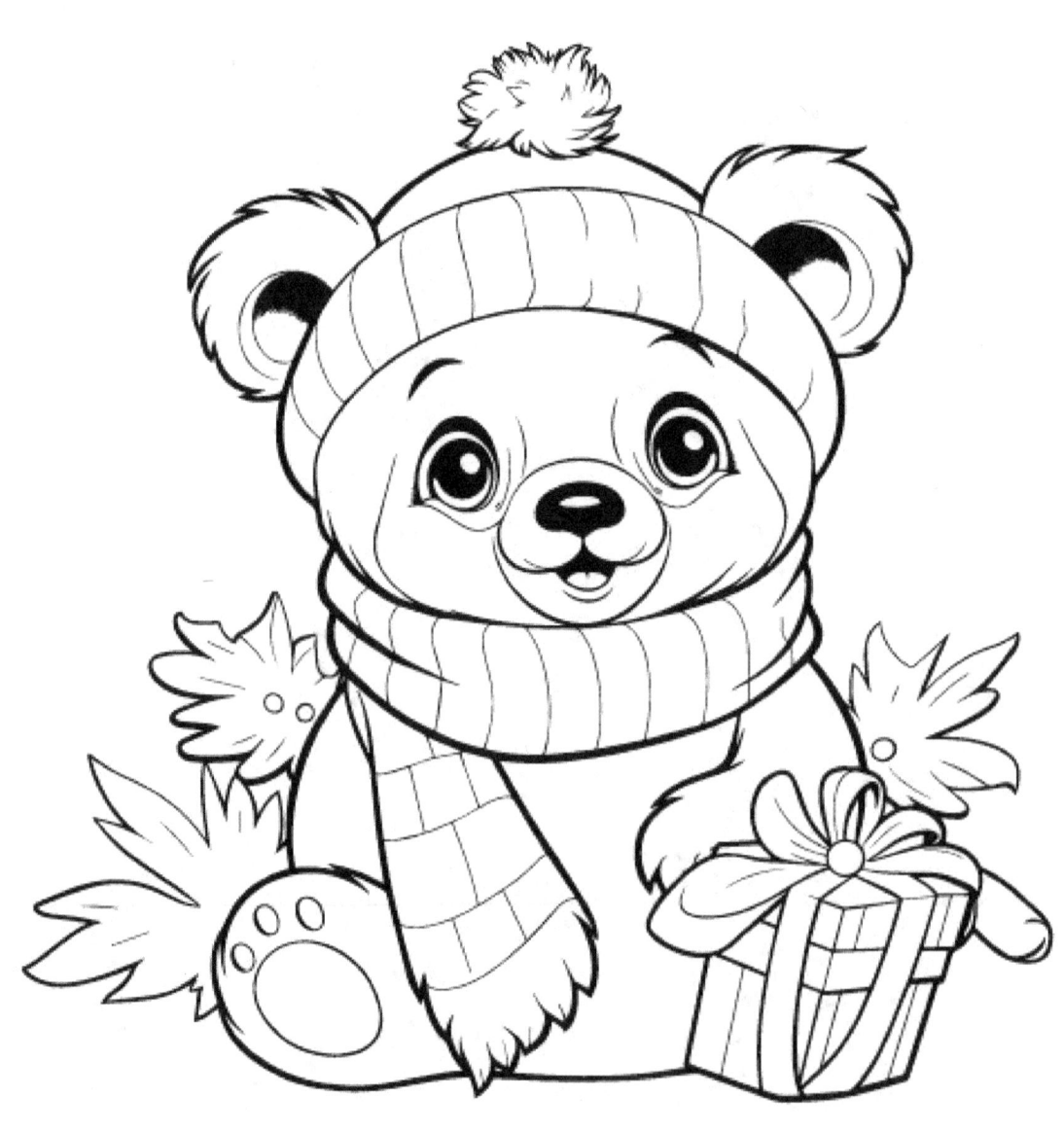

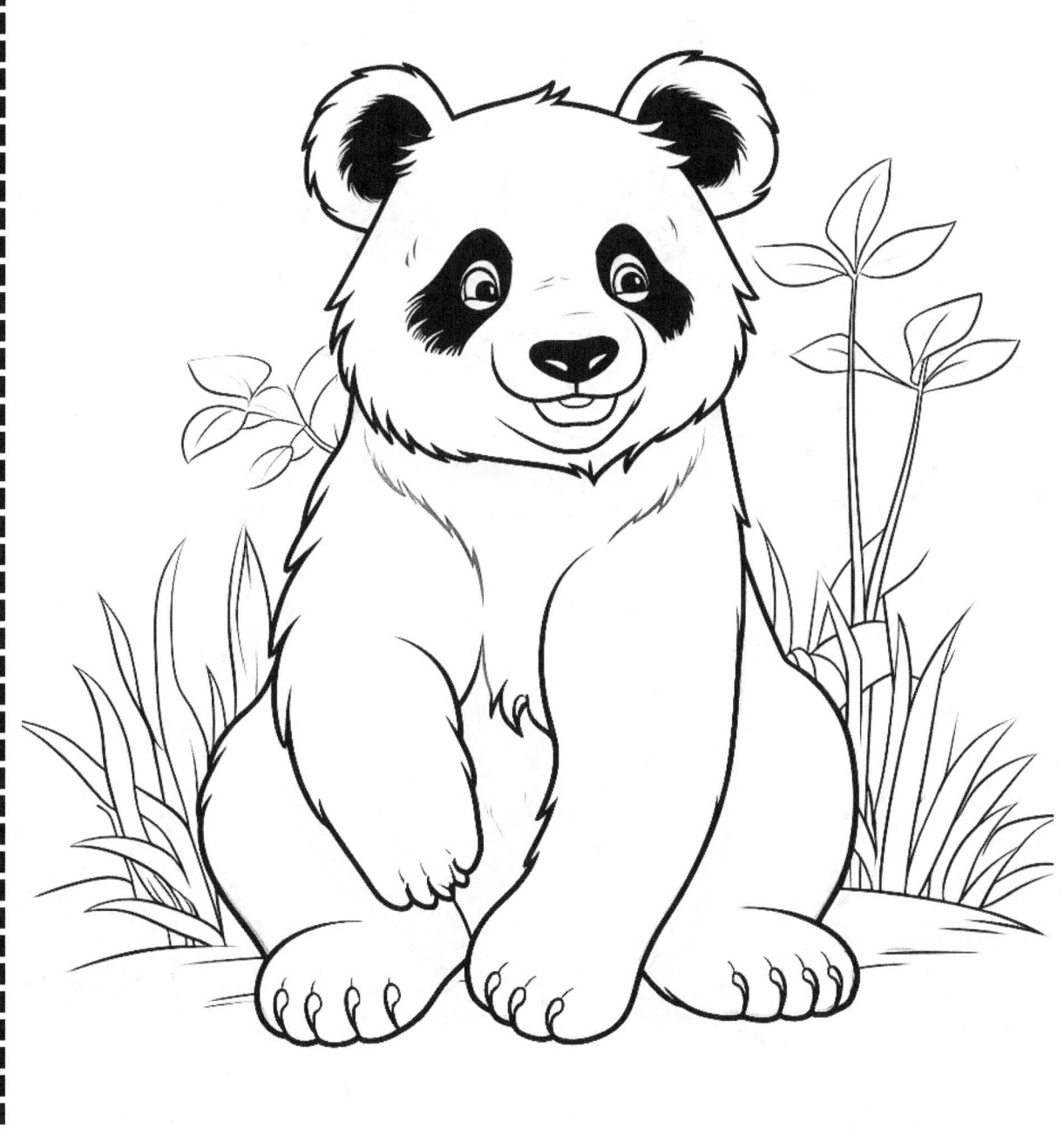

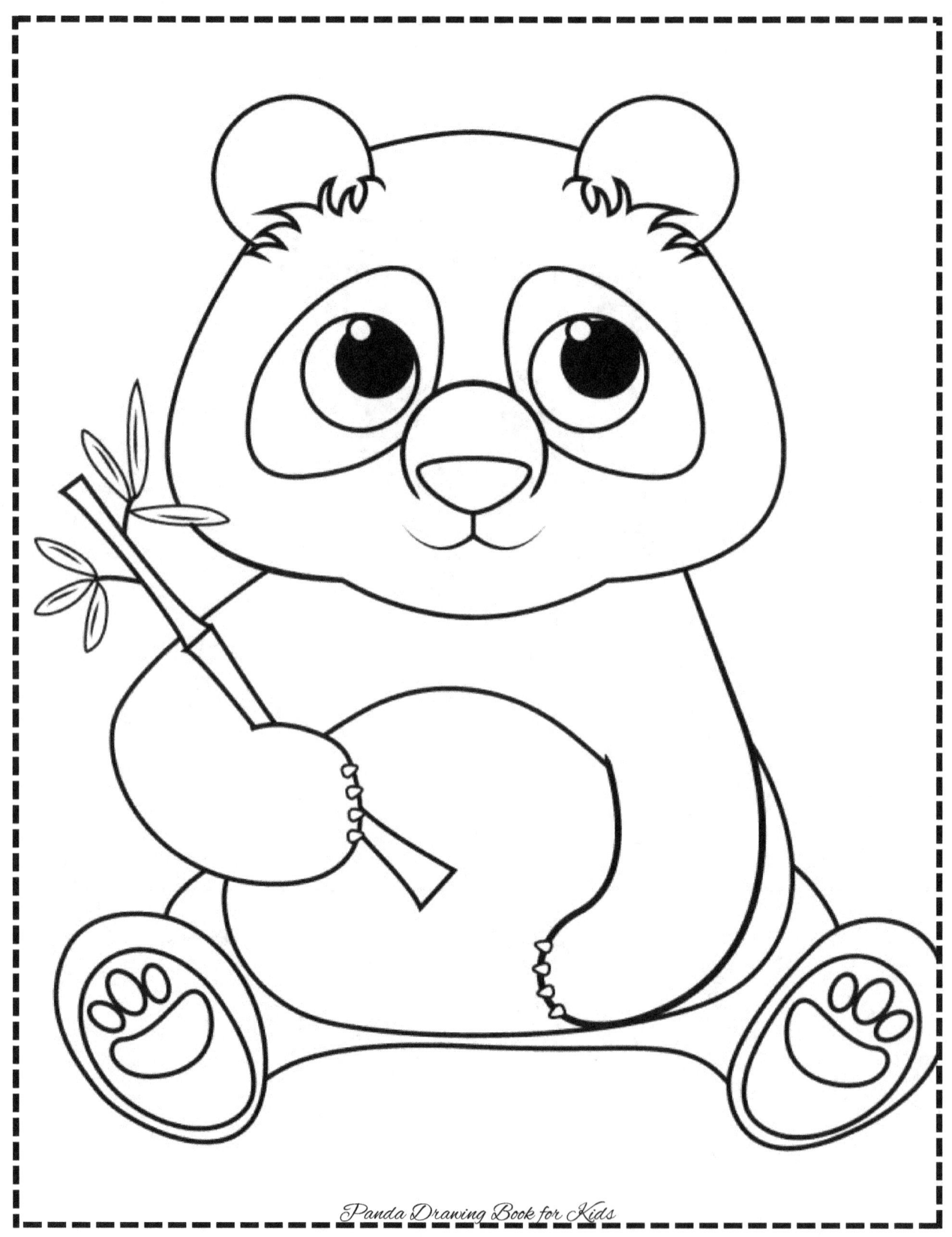

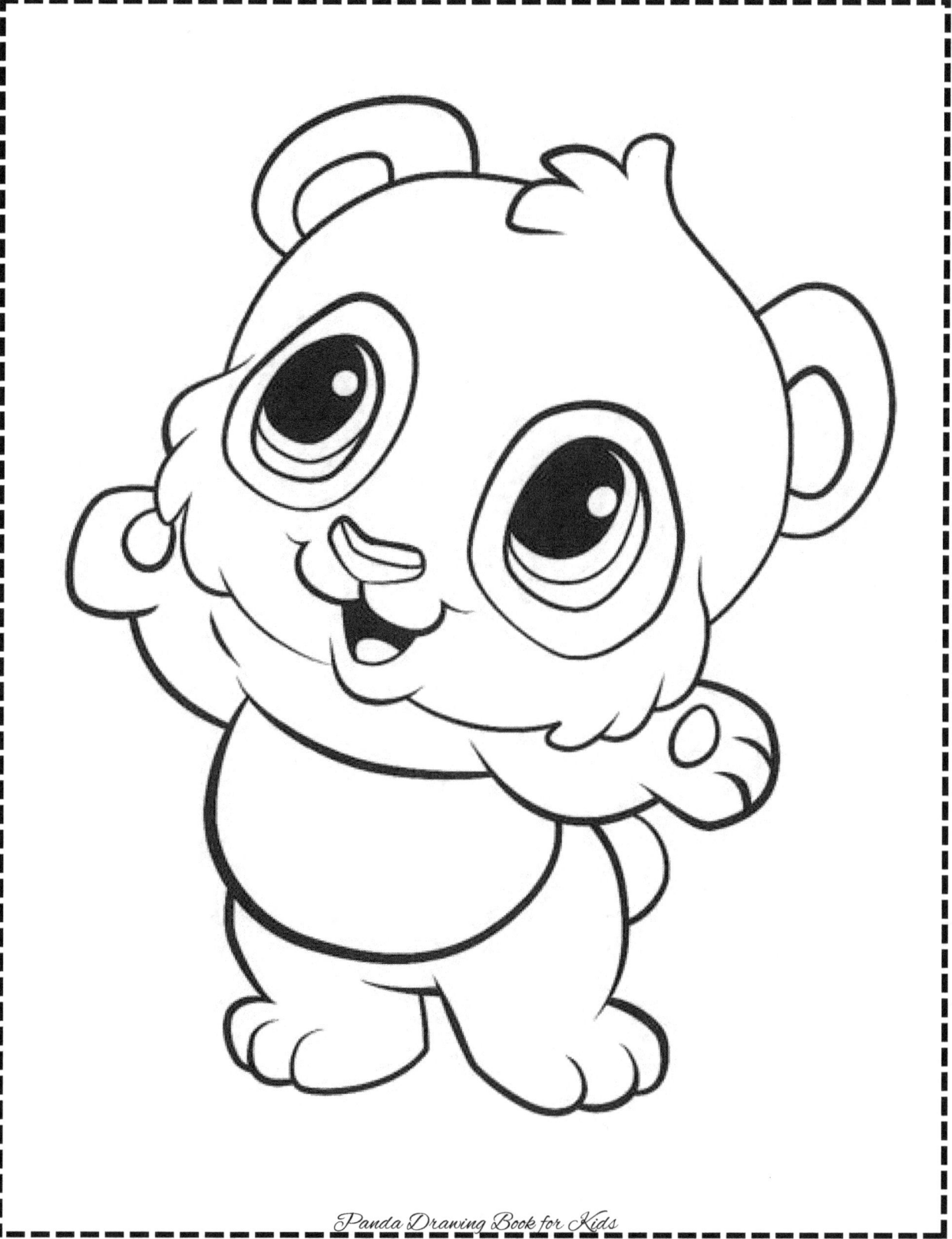

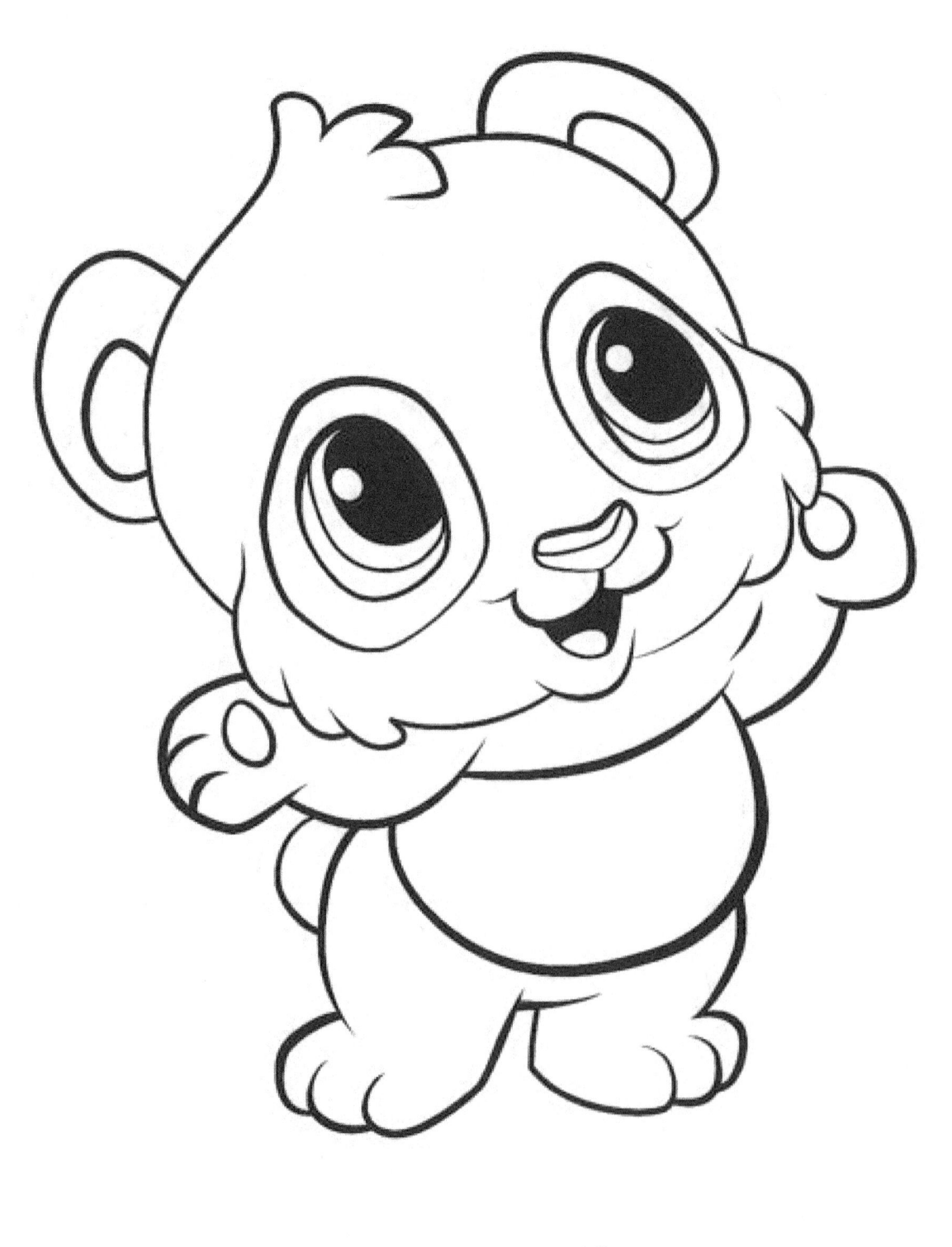
Panda Drawing Book for Kids

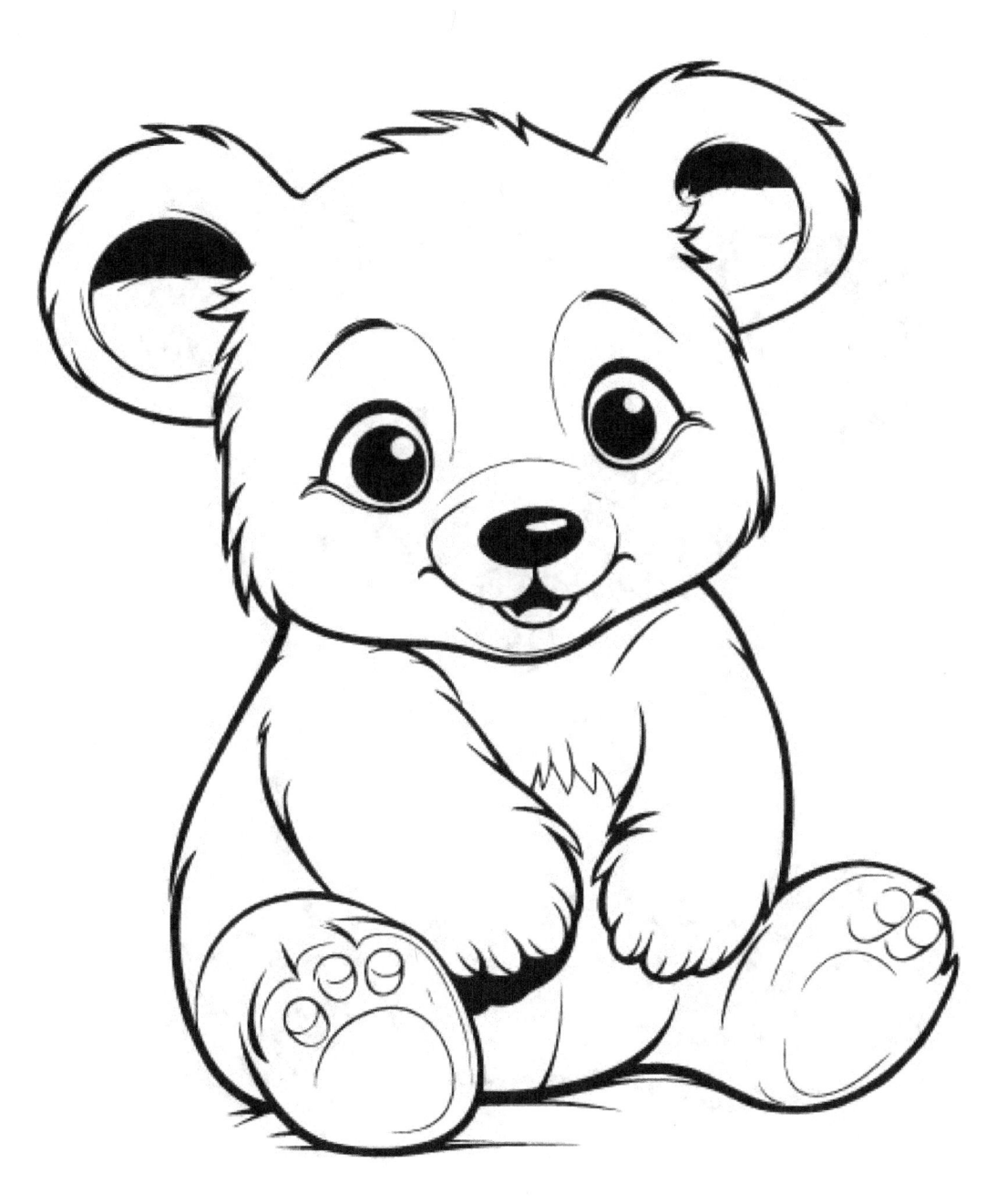

Panda Drawing Book for Kids

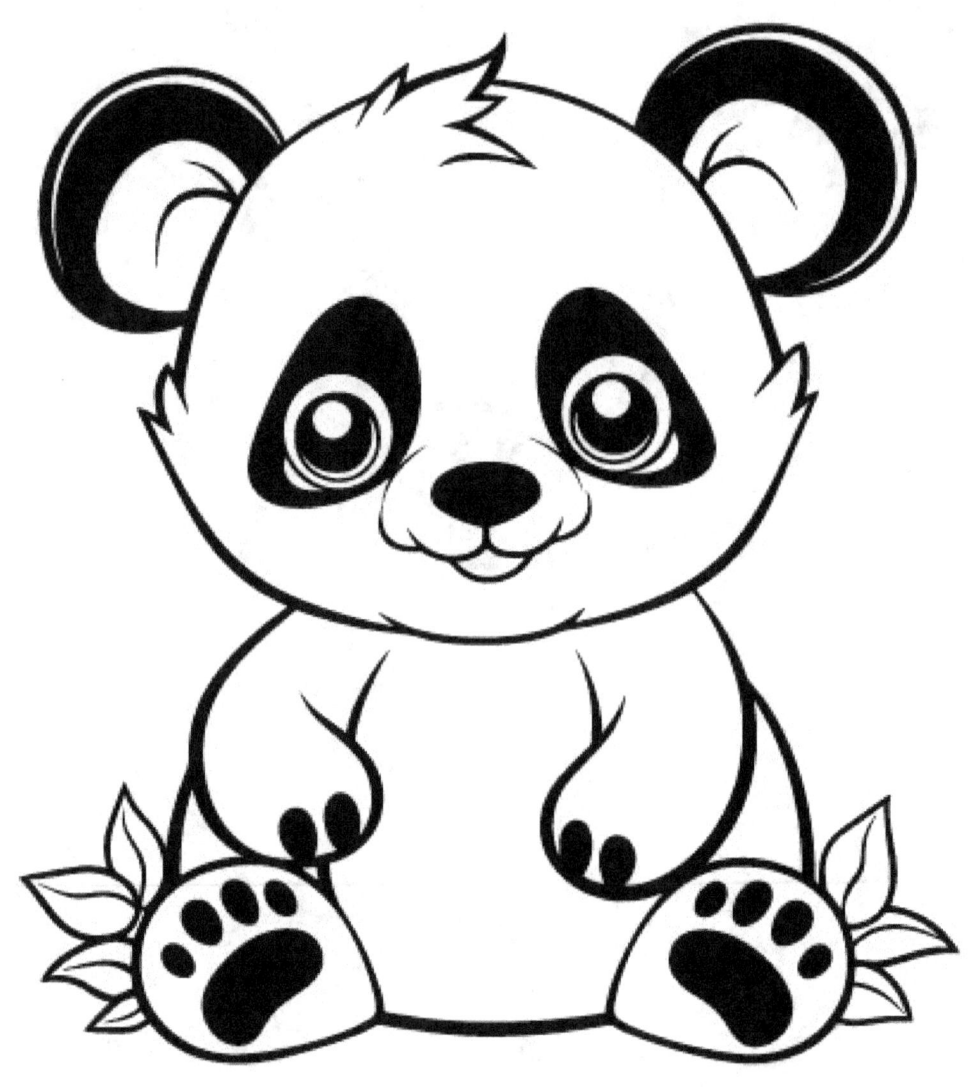

Panda Drawing Book for Kids

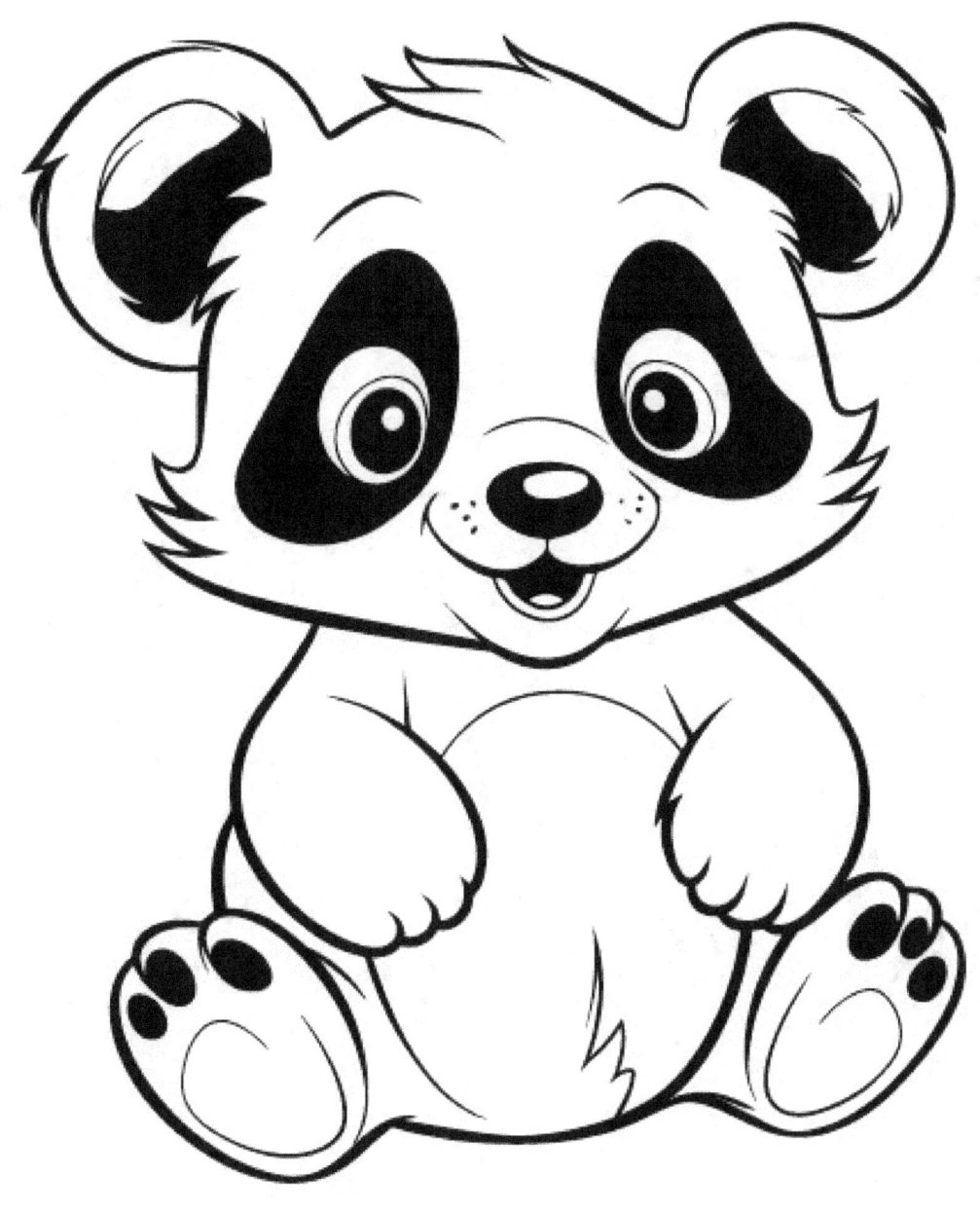

Panda Drawing Book for Kids

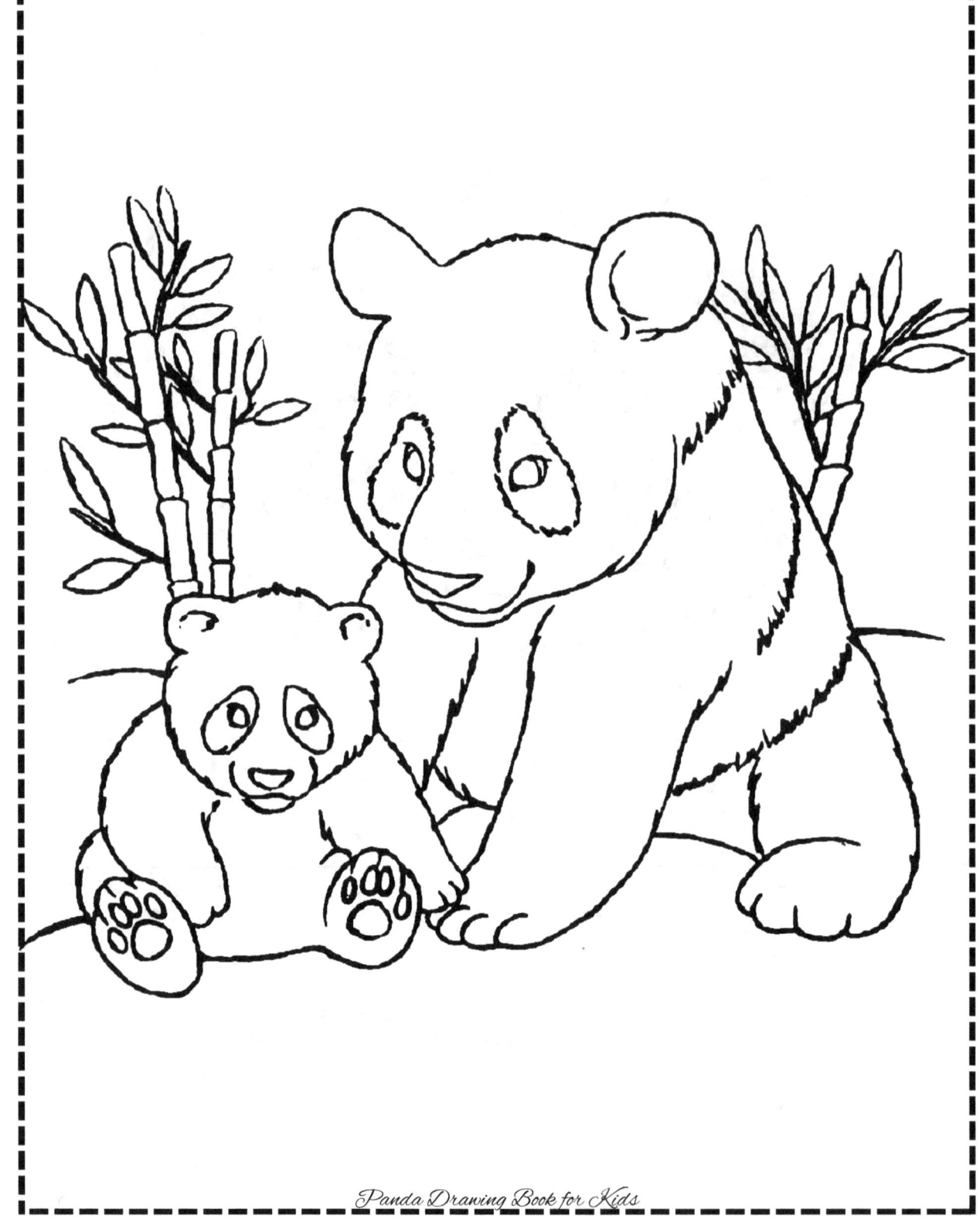

Panda Drawing Book for Kids

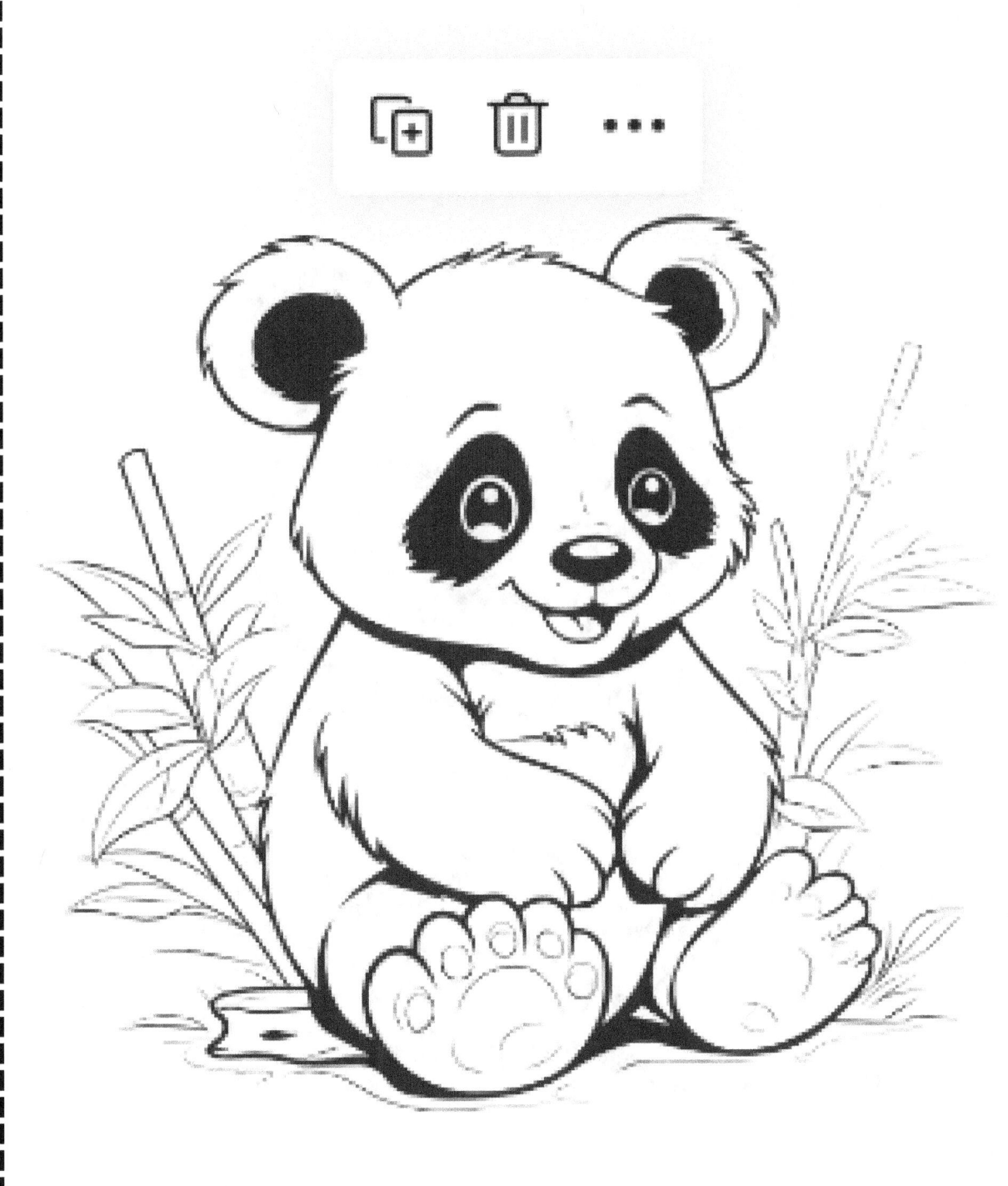

Panda Drawing Book for Kids

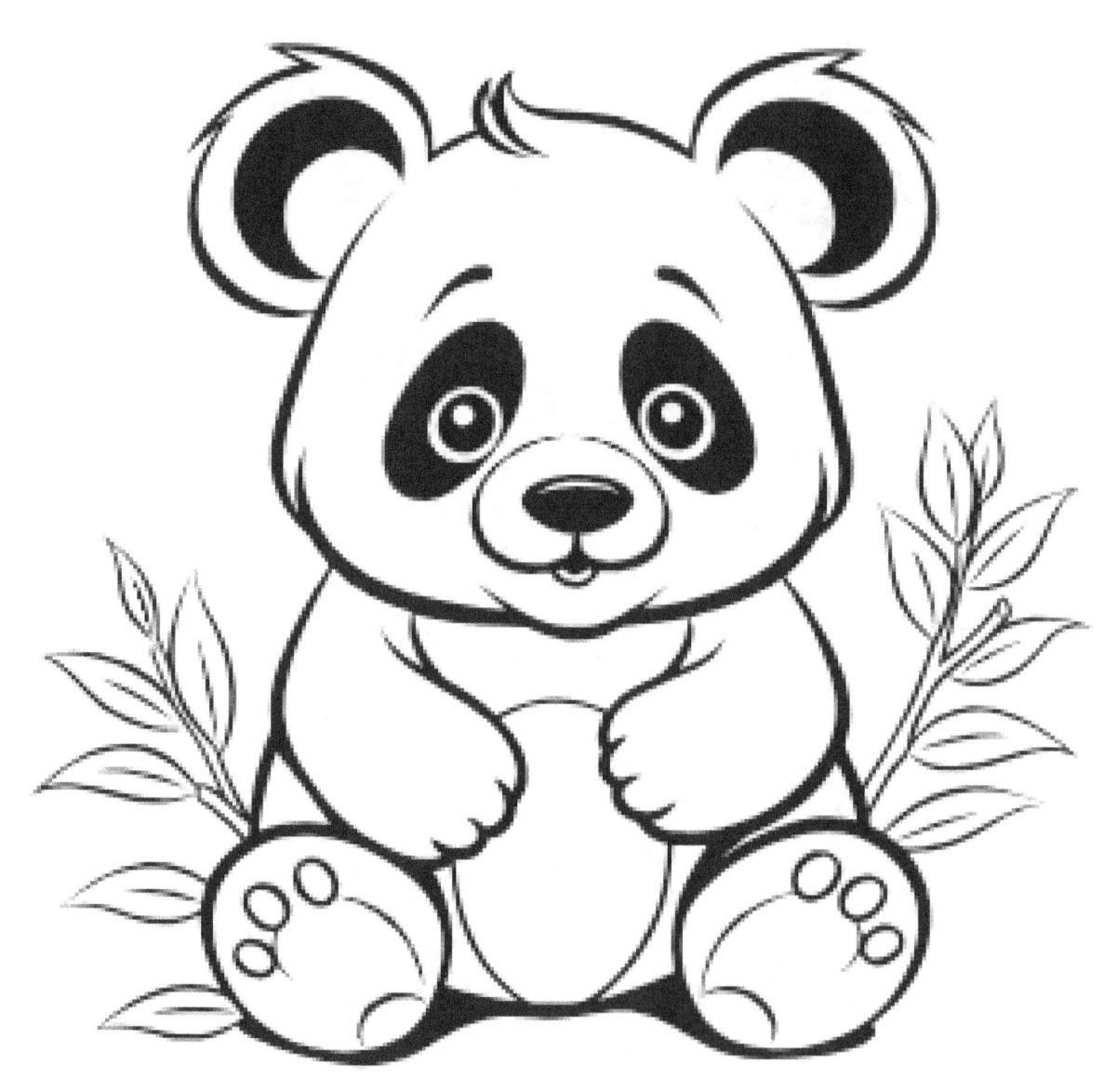

Panda Drawing Book for Kids

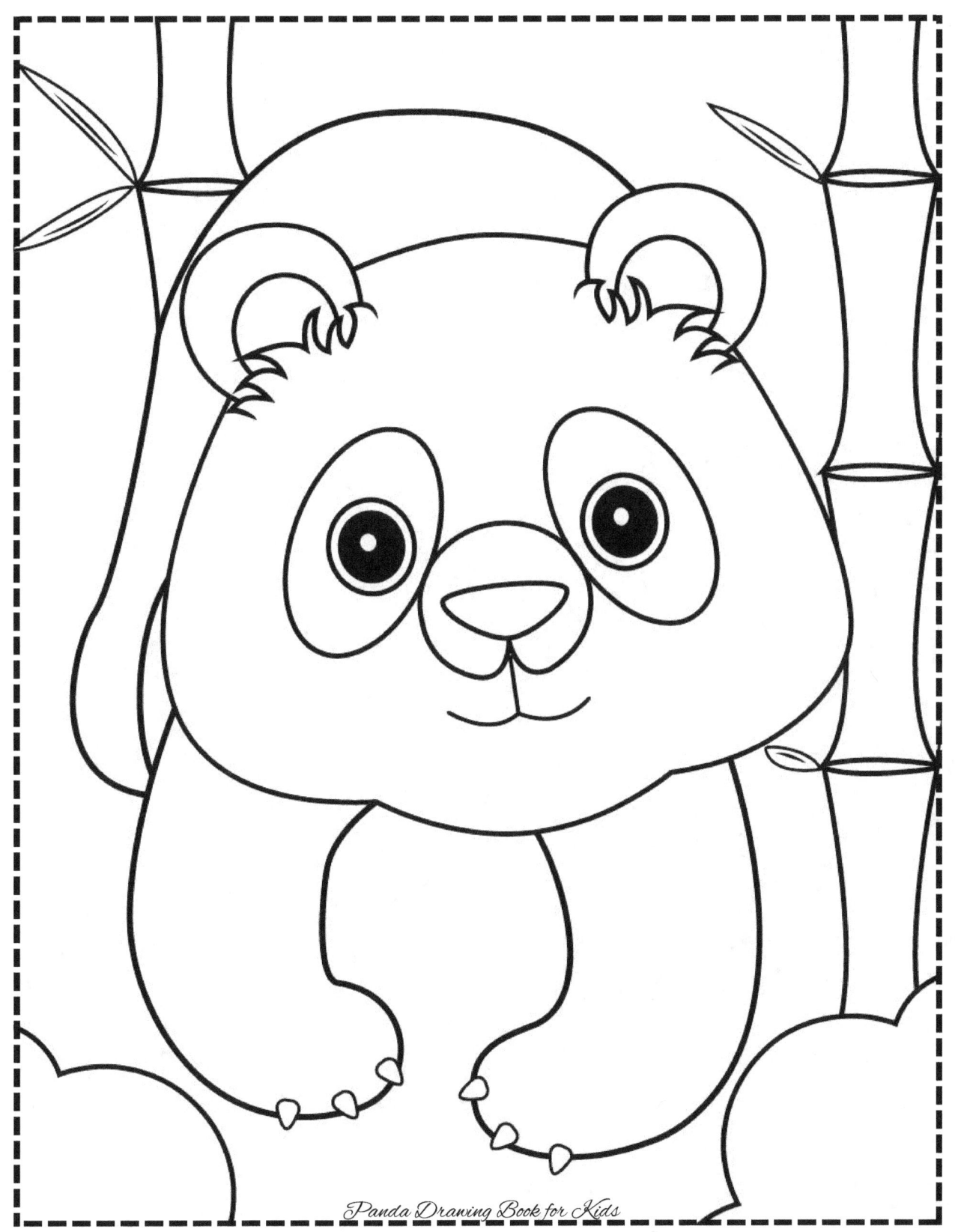
Panda Drawing Book for Kids

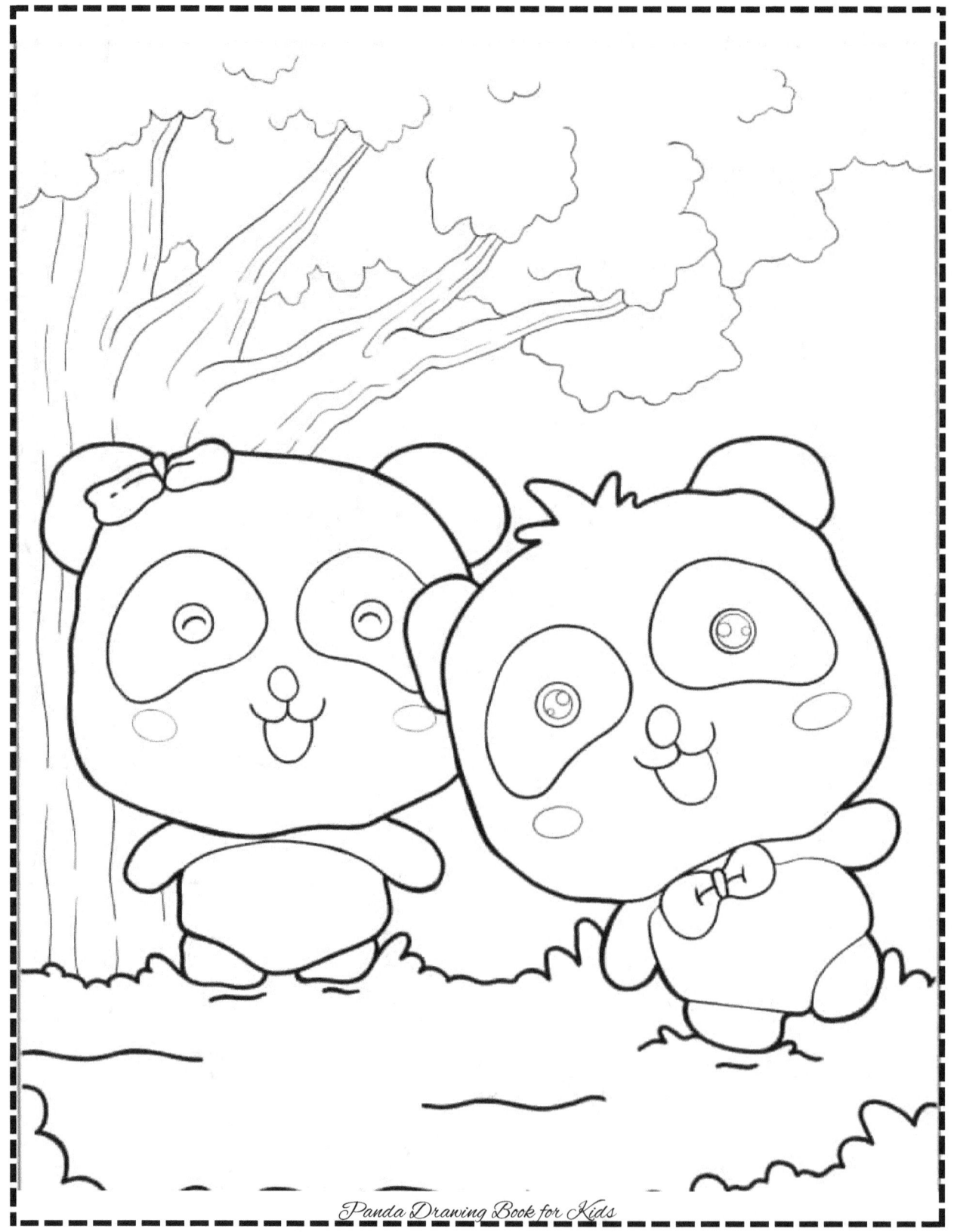

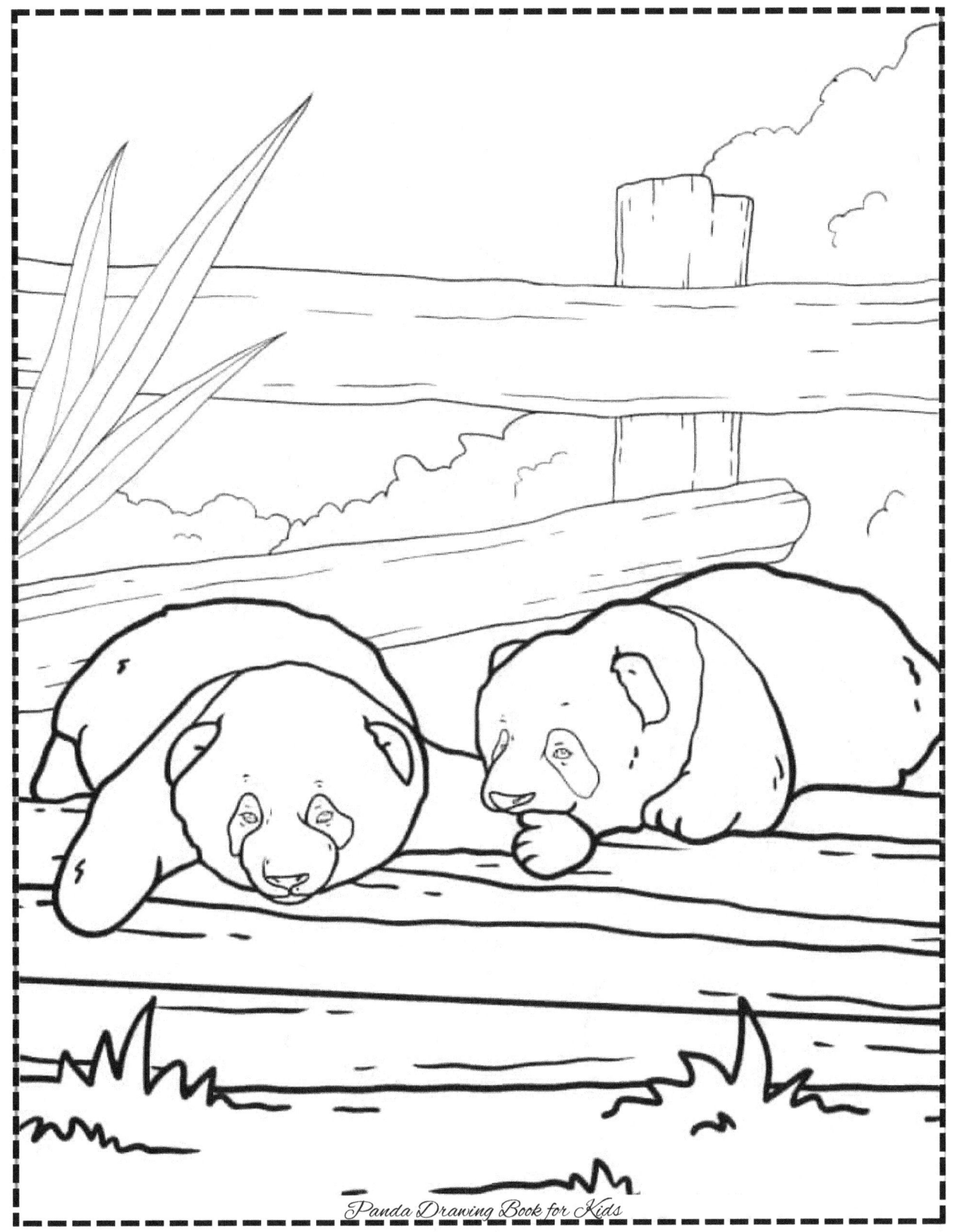

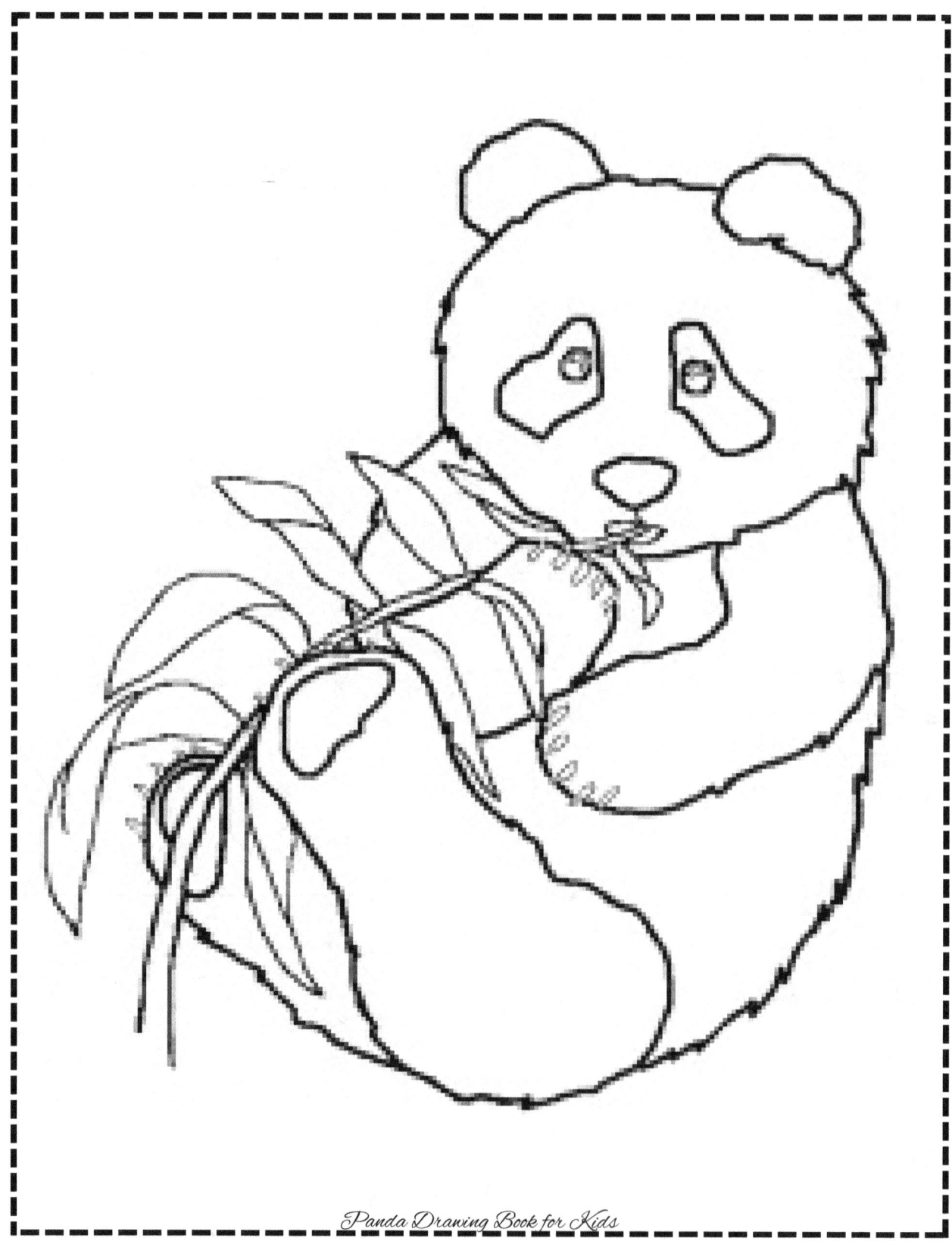

Panda Drawing Book for Kids

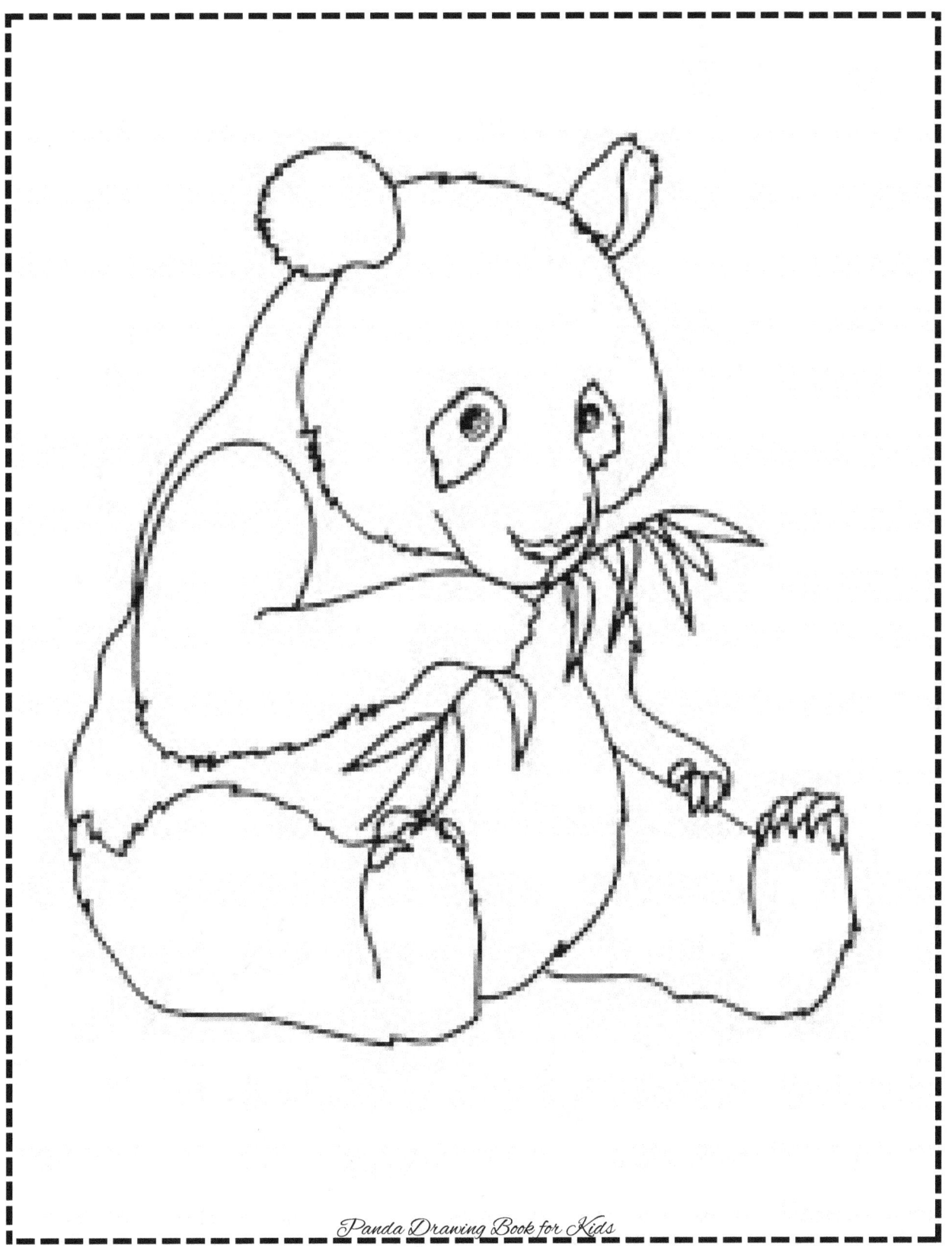
Panda Drawing Book for Kids

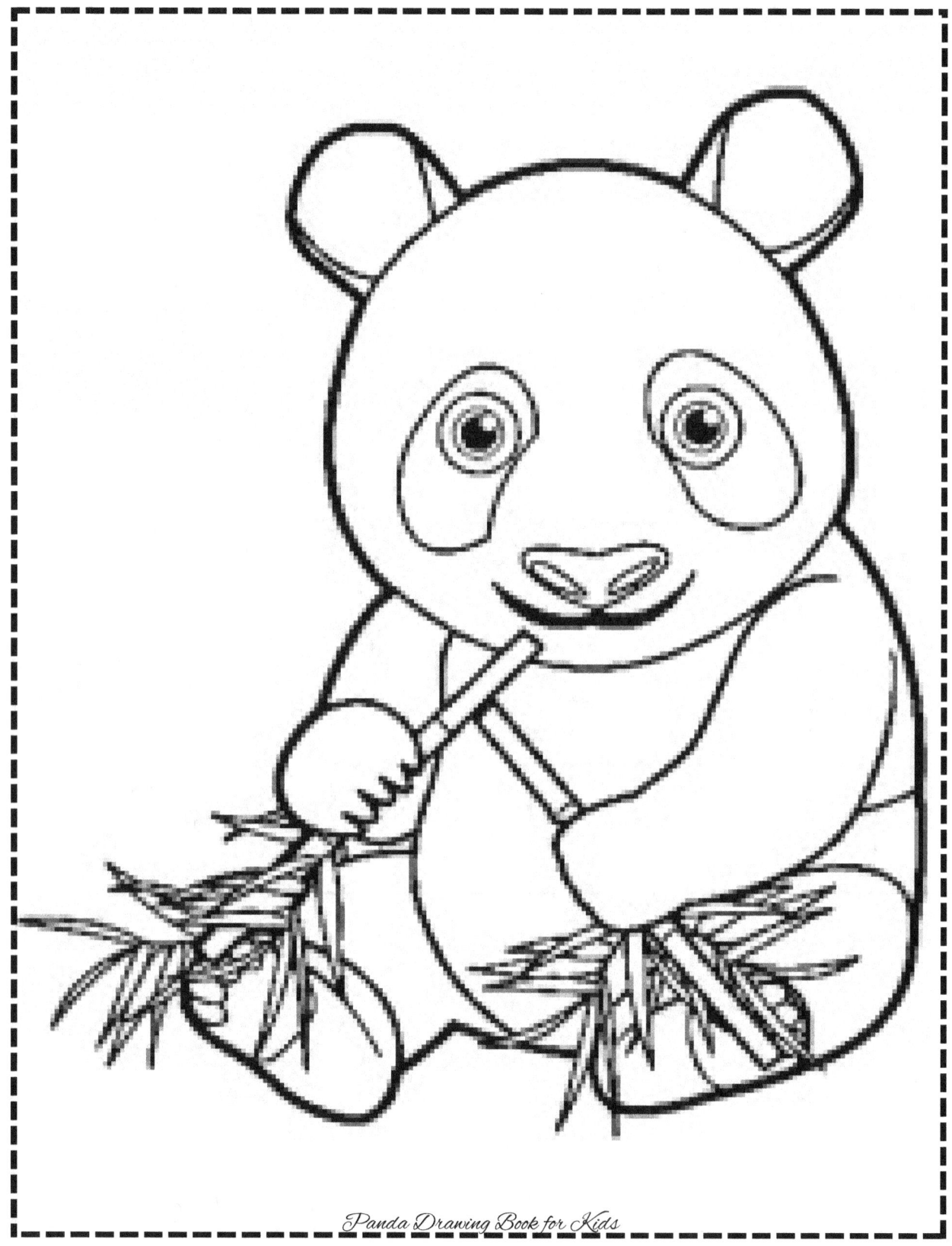

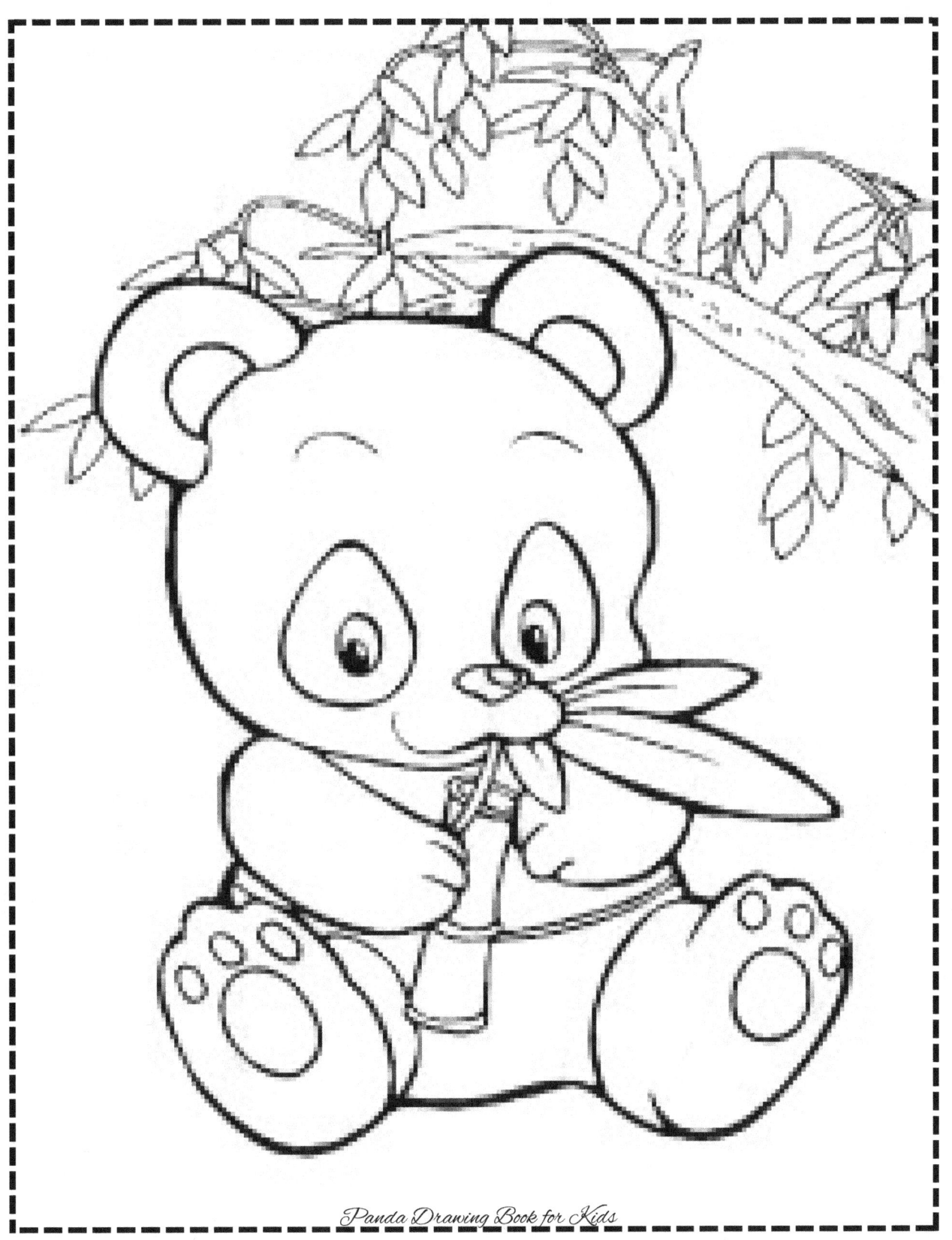

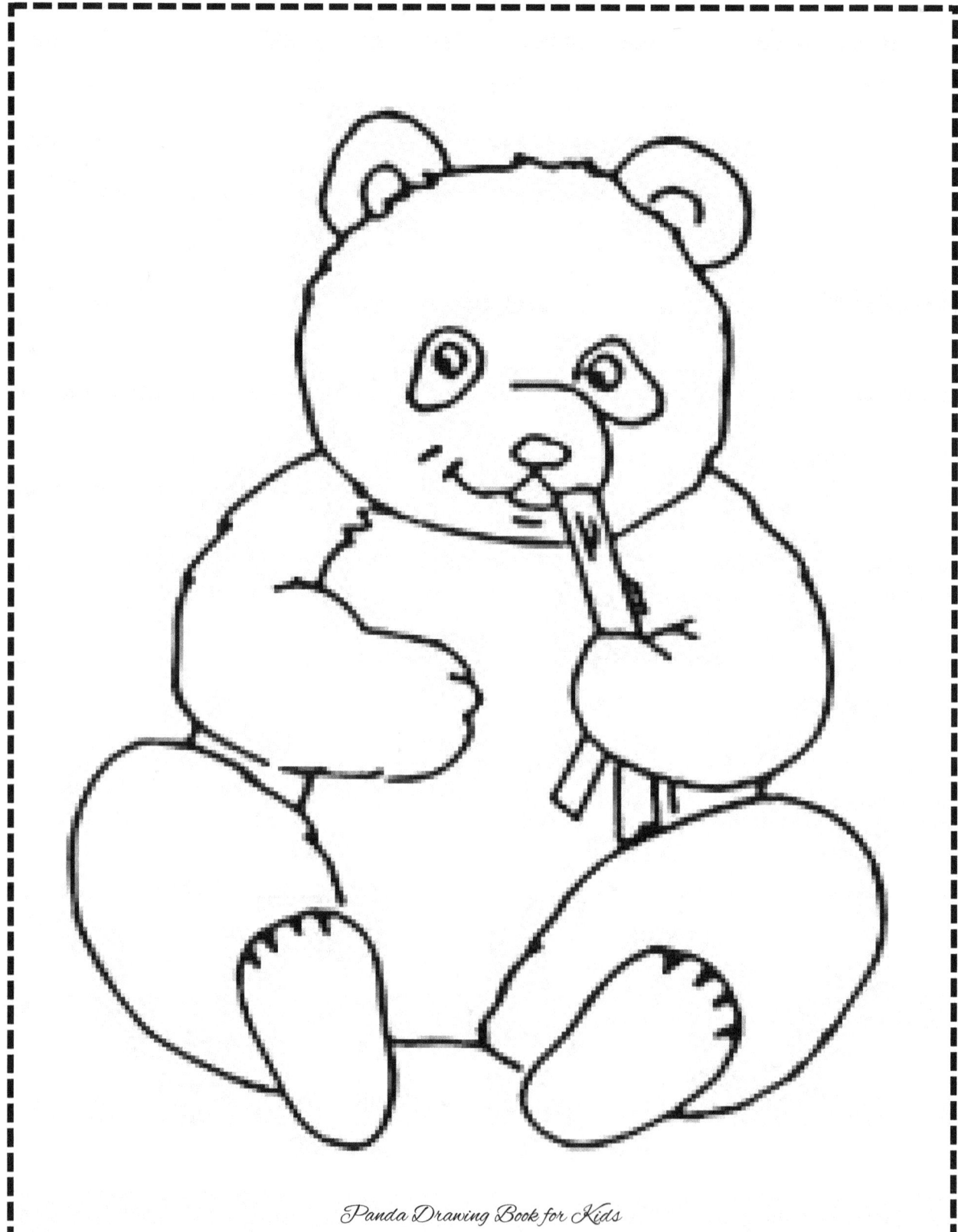

Panda Drawing Book for Kids

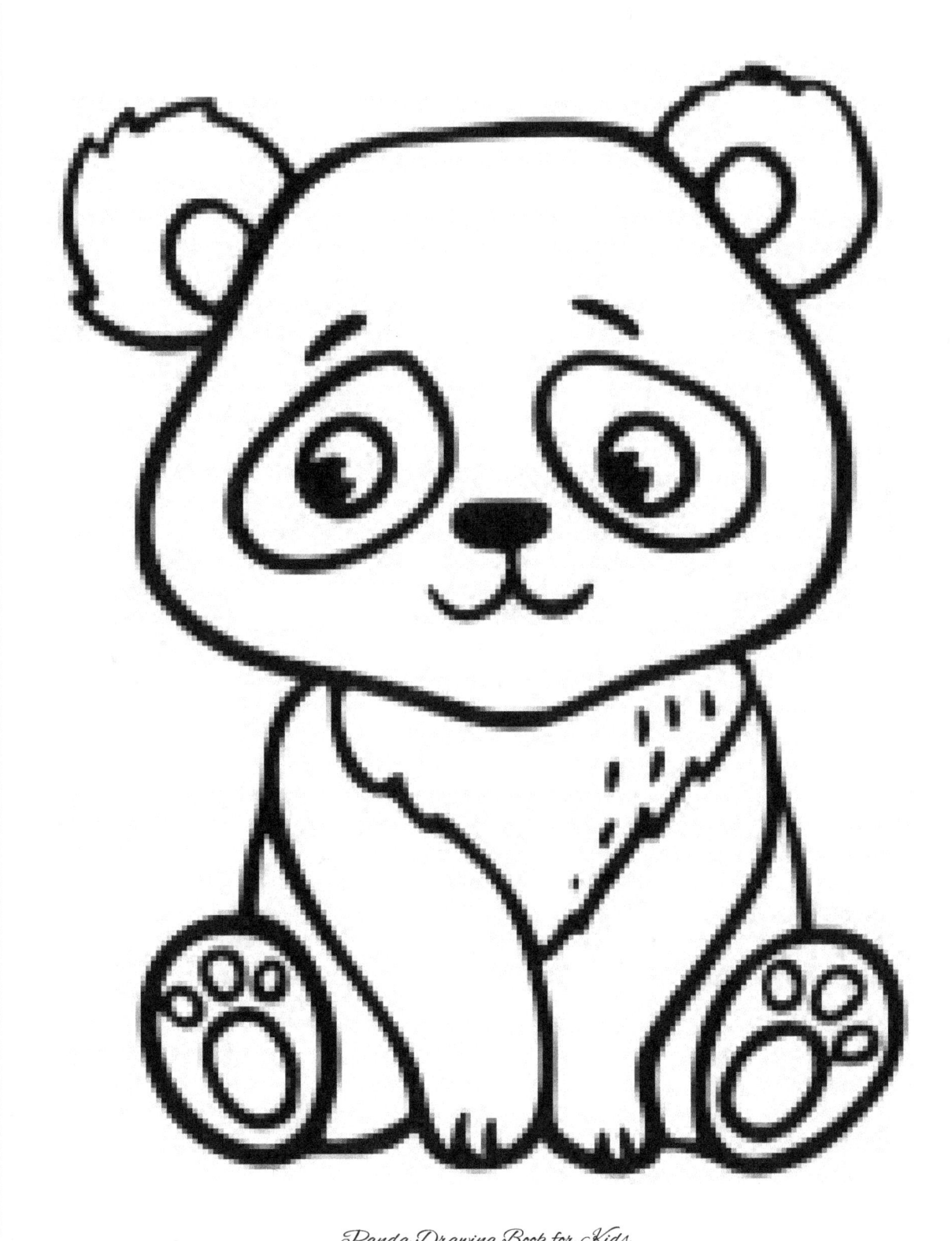

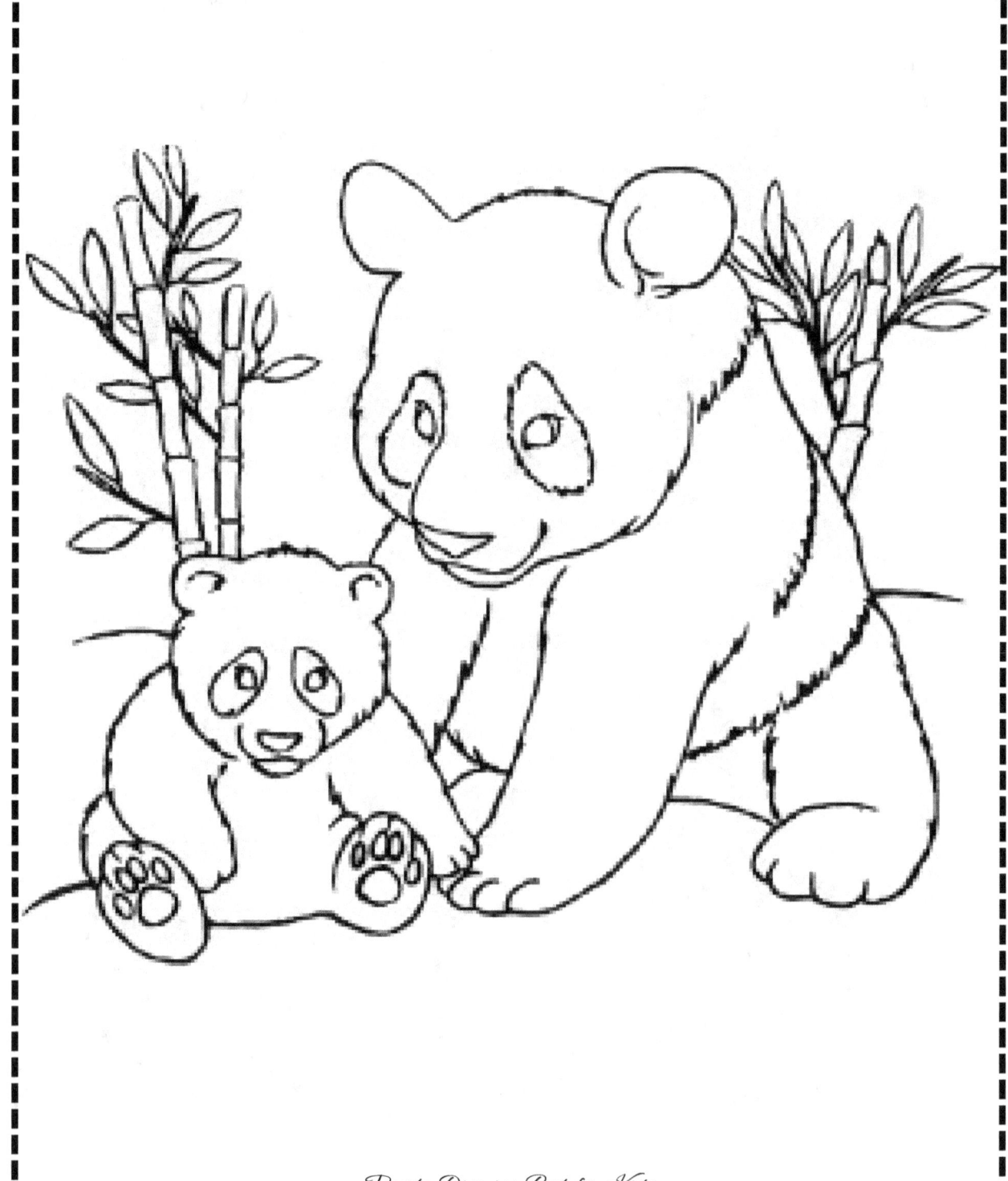

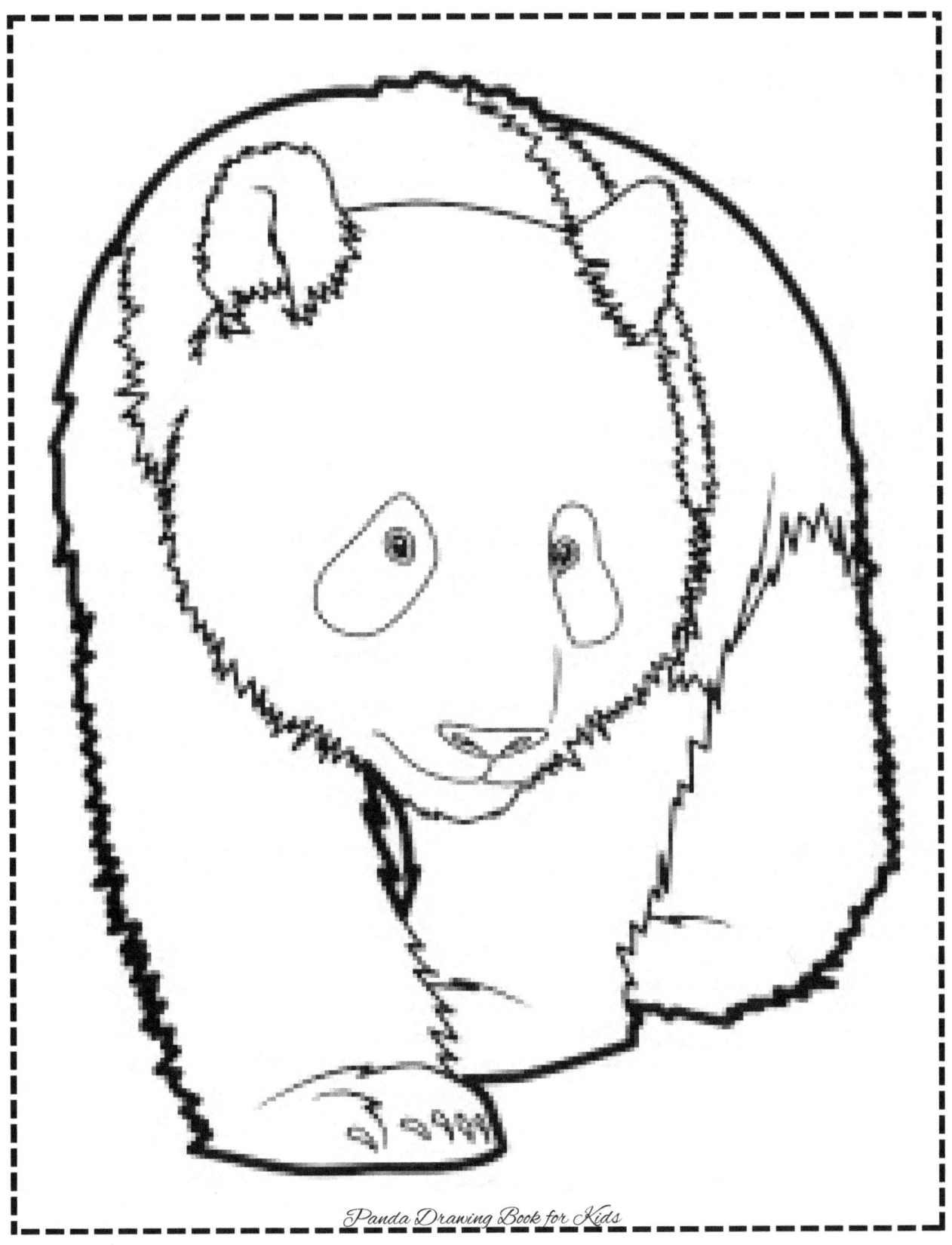
Panda Drawing Book for Kids

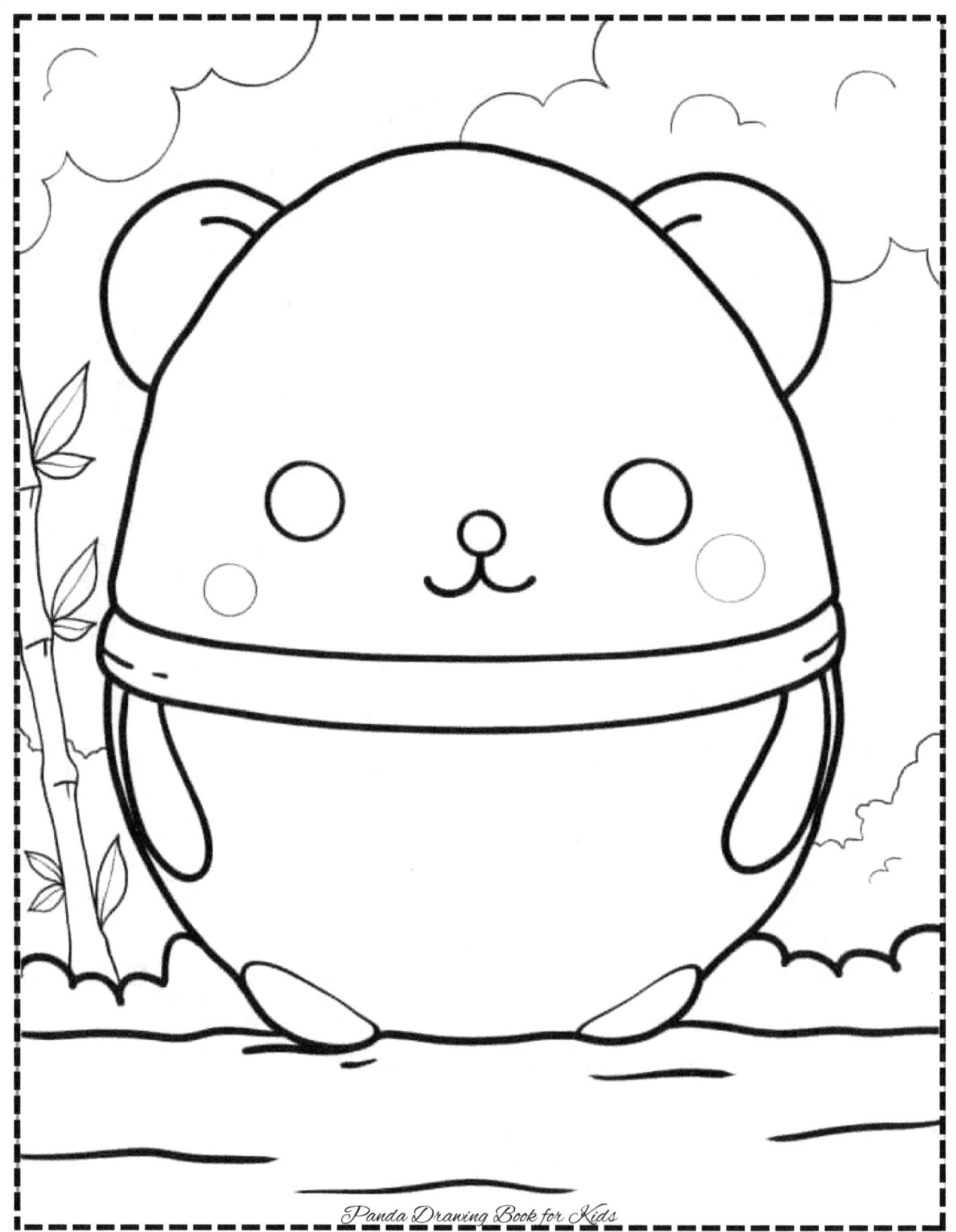

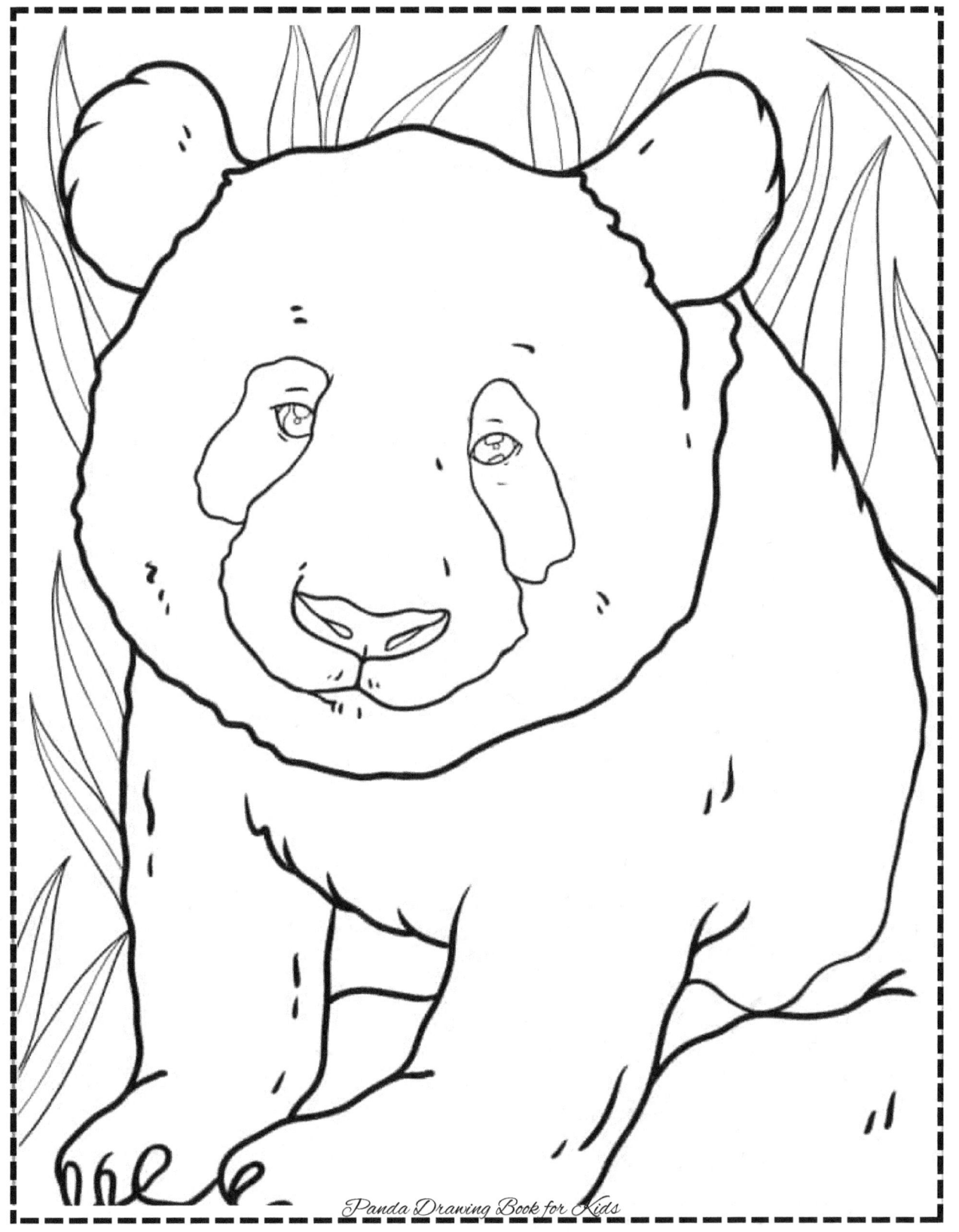

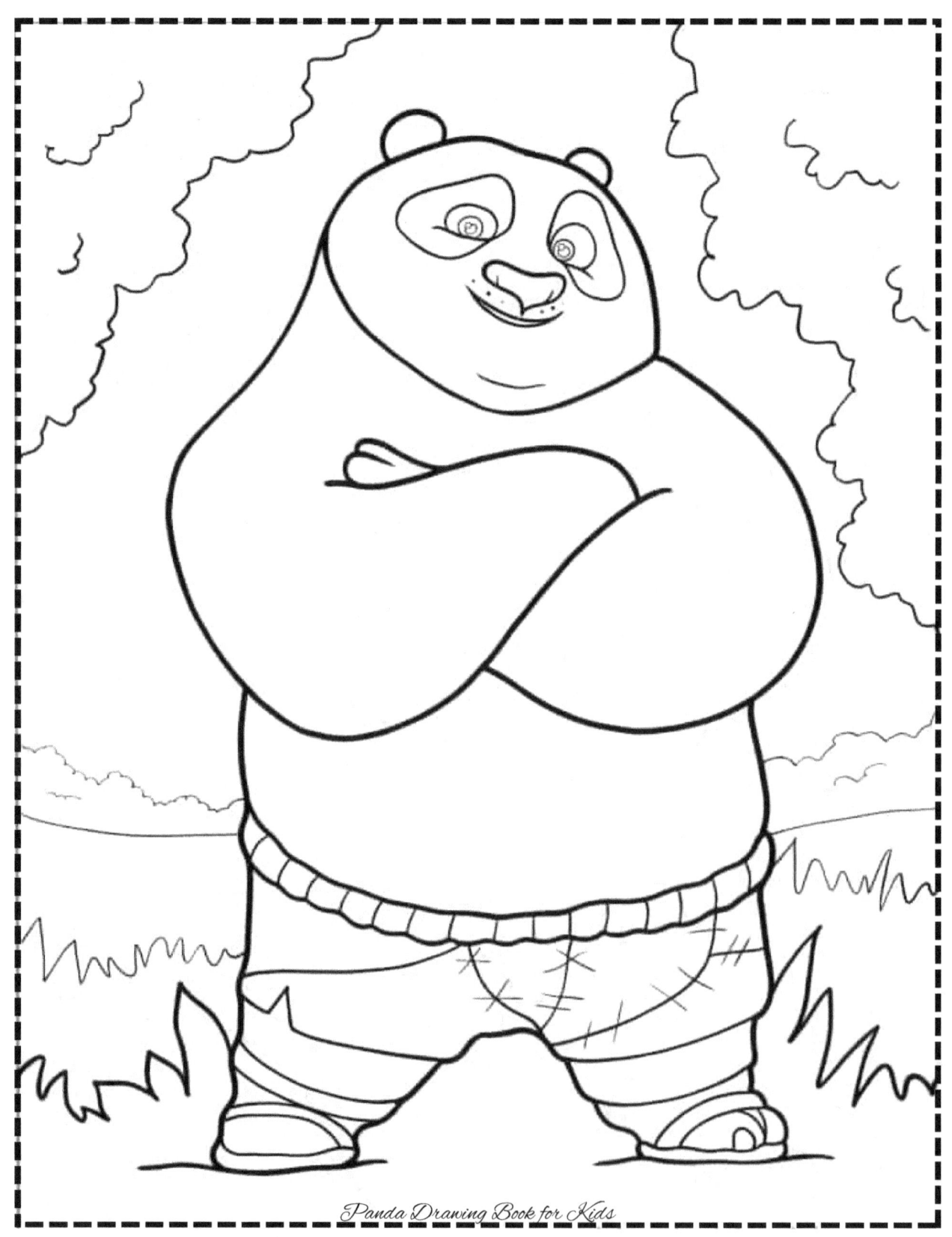

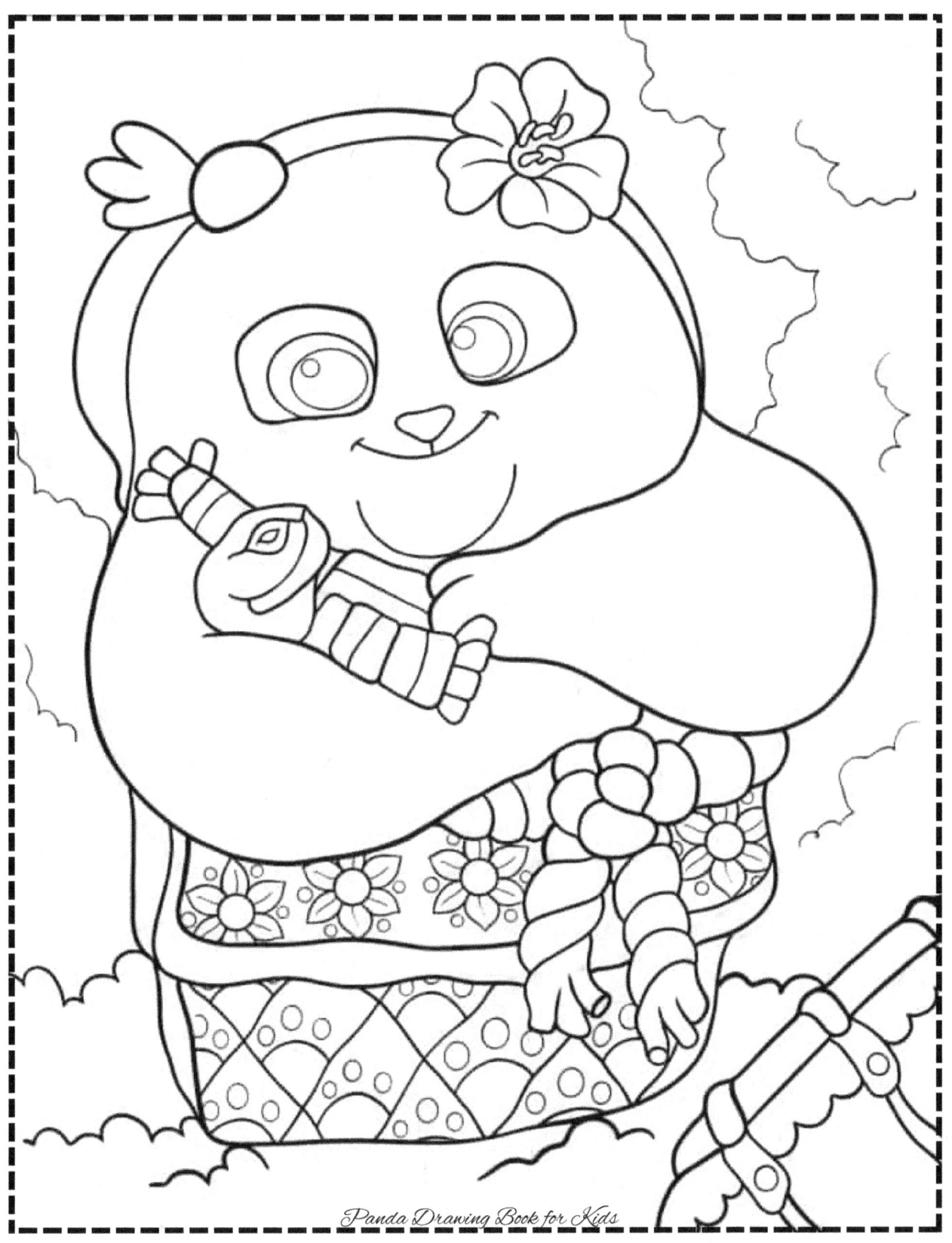

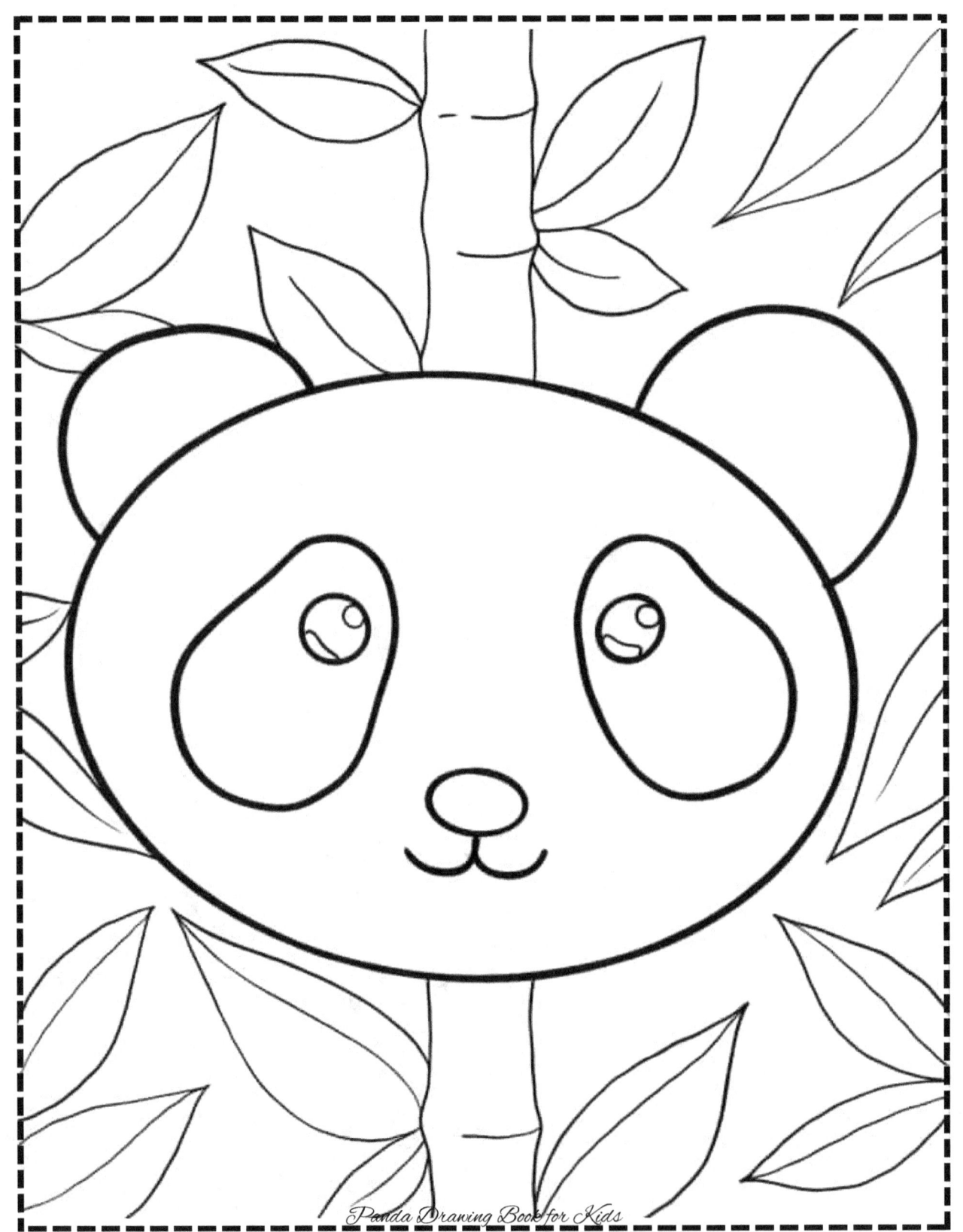

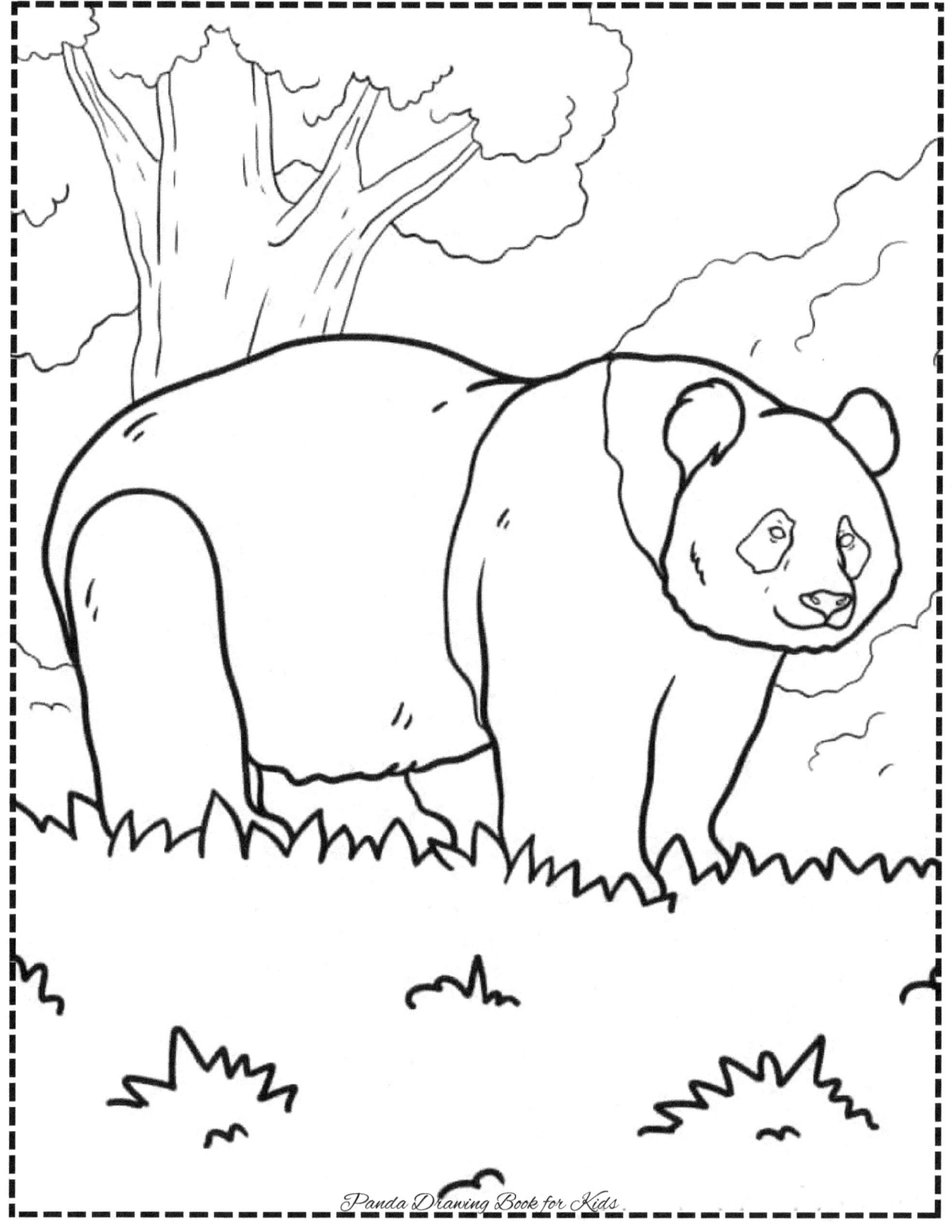

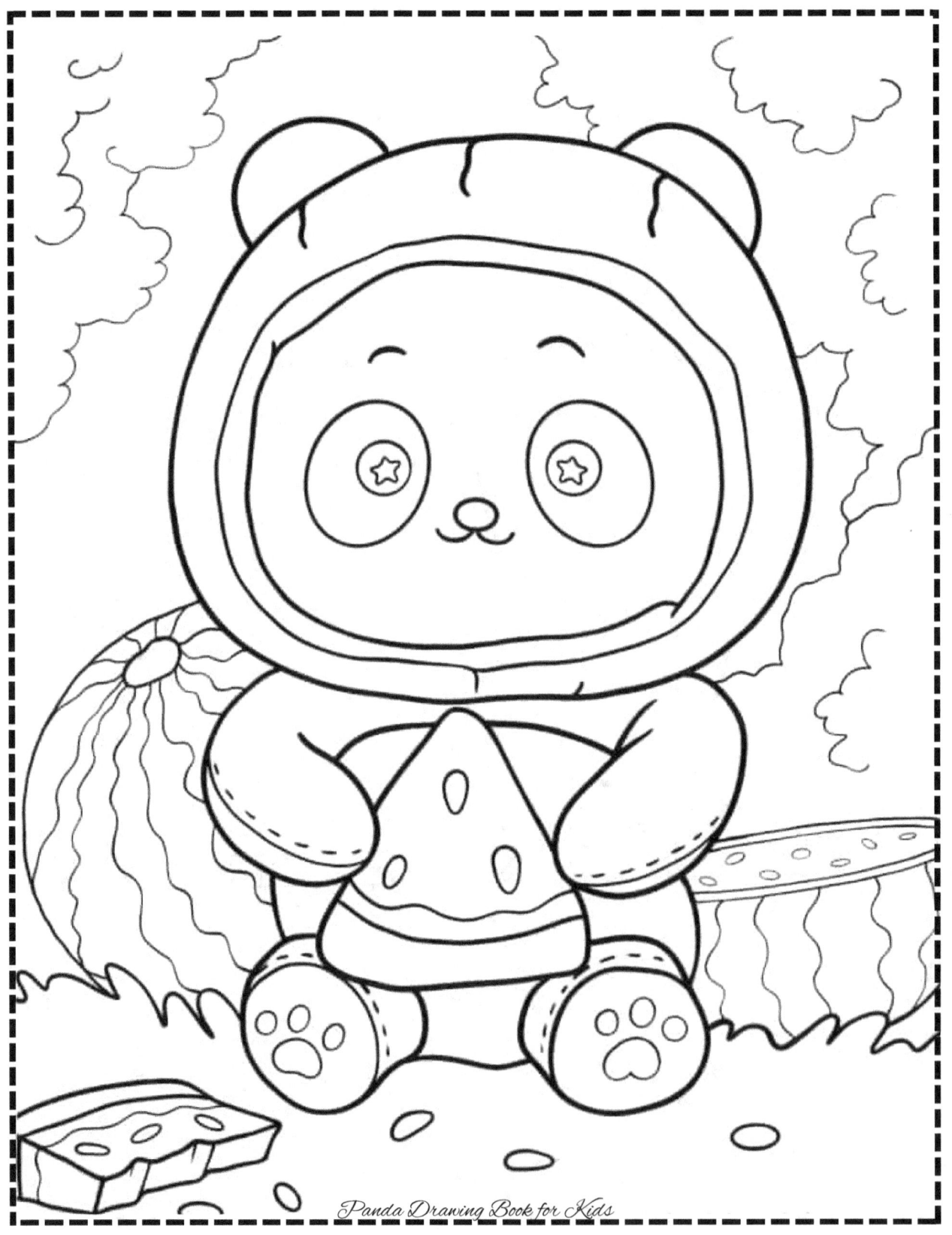

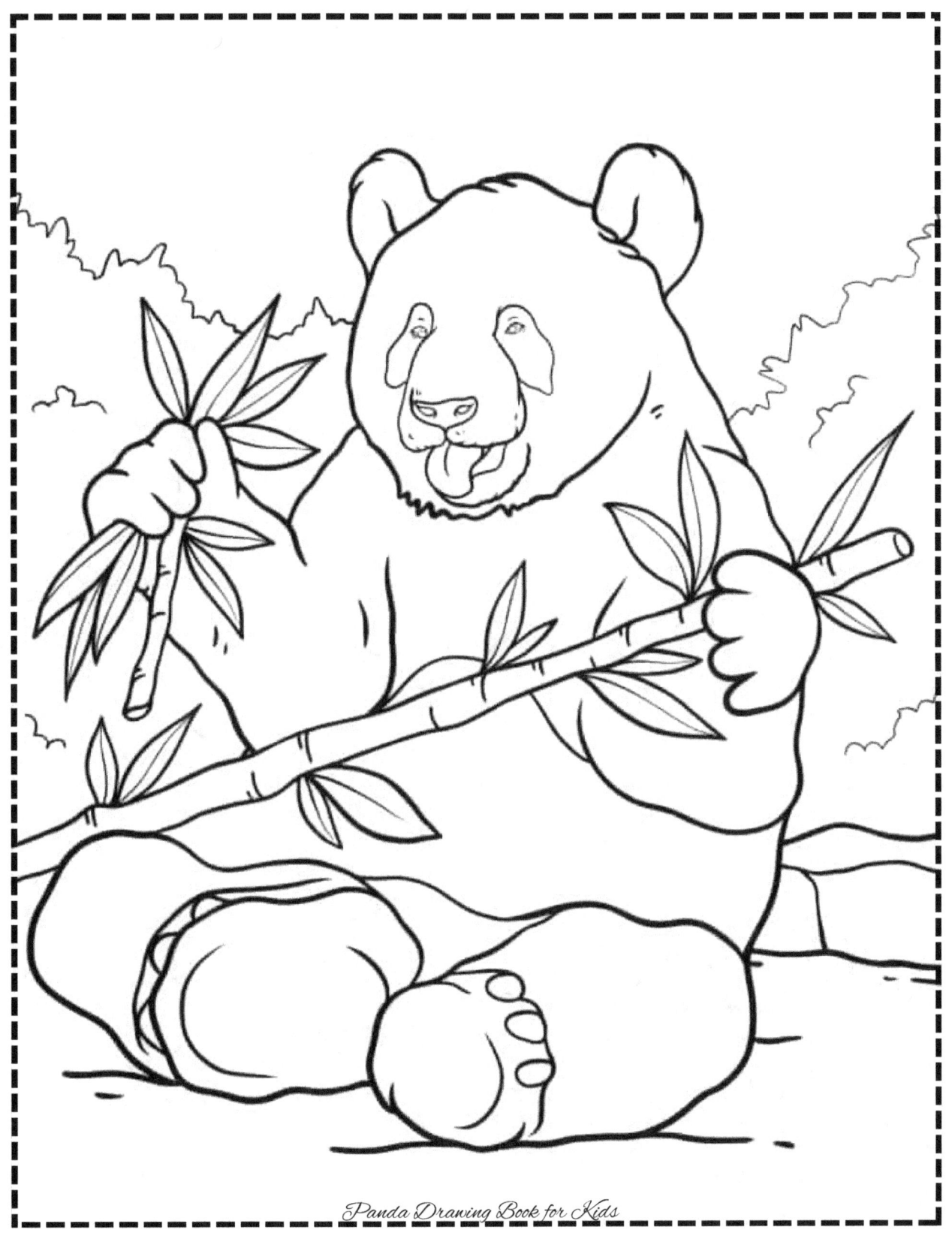

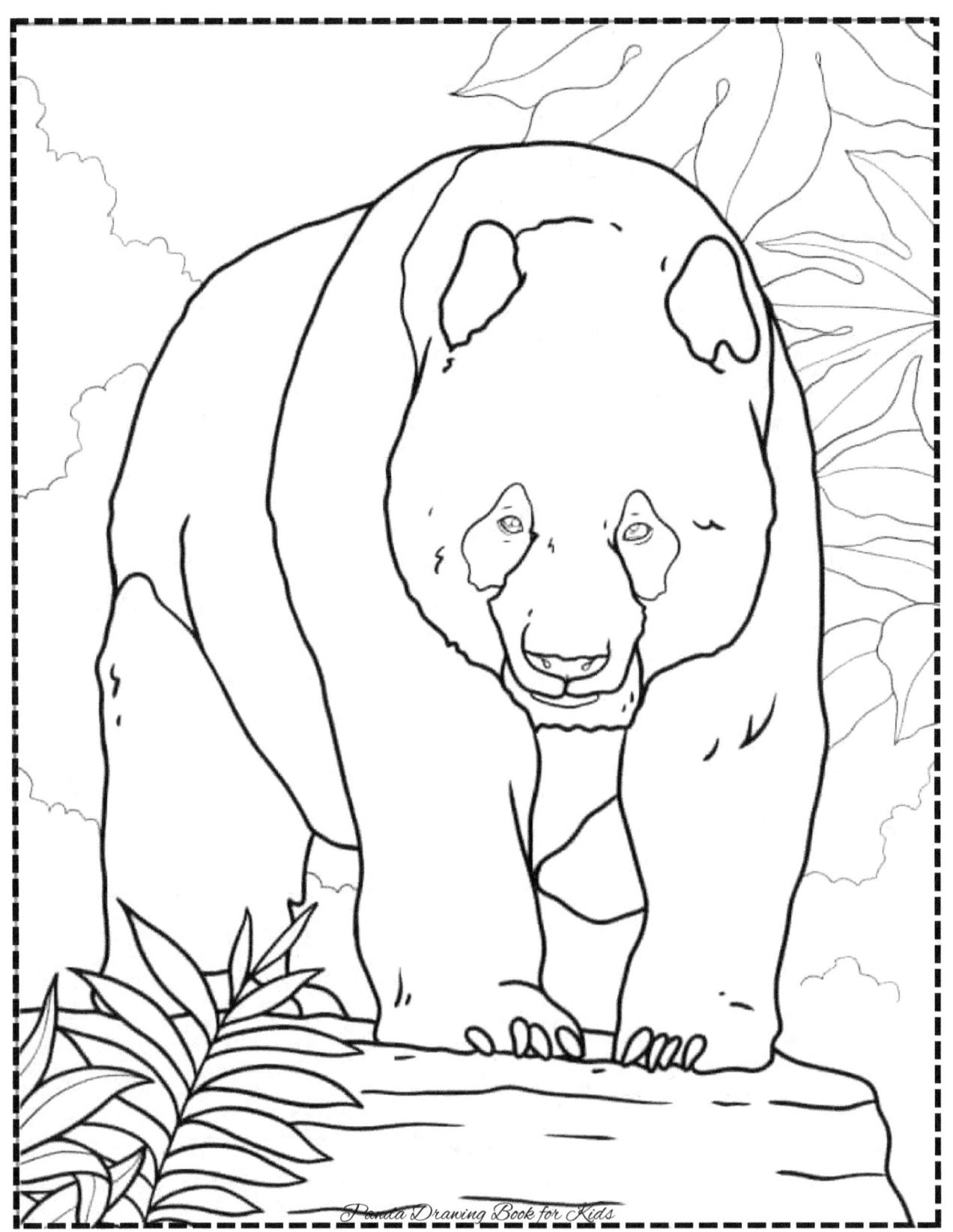

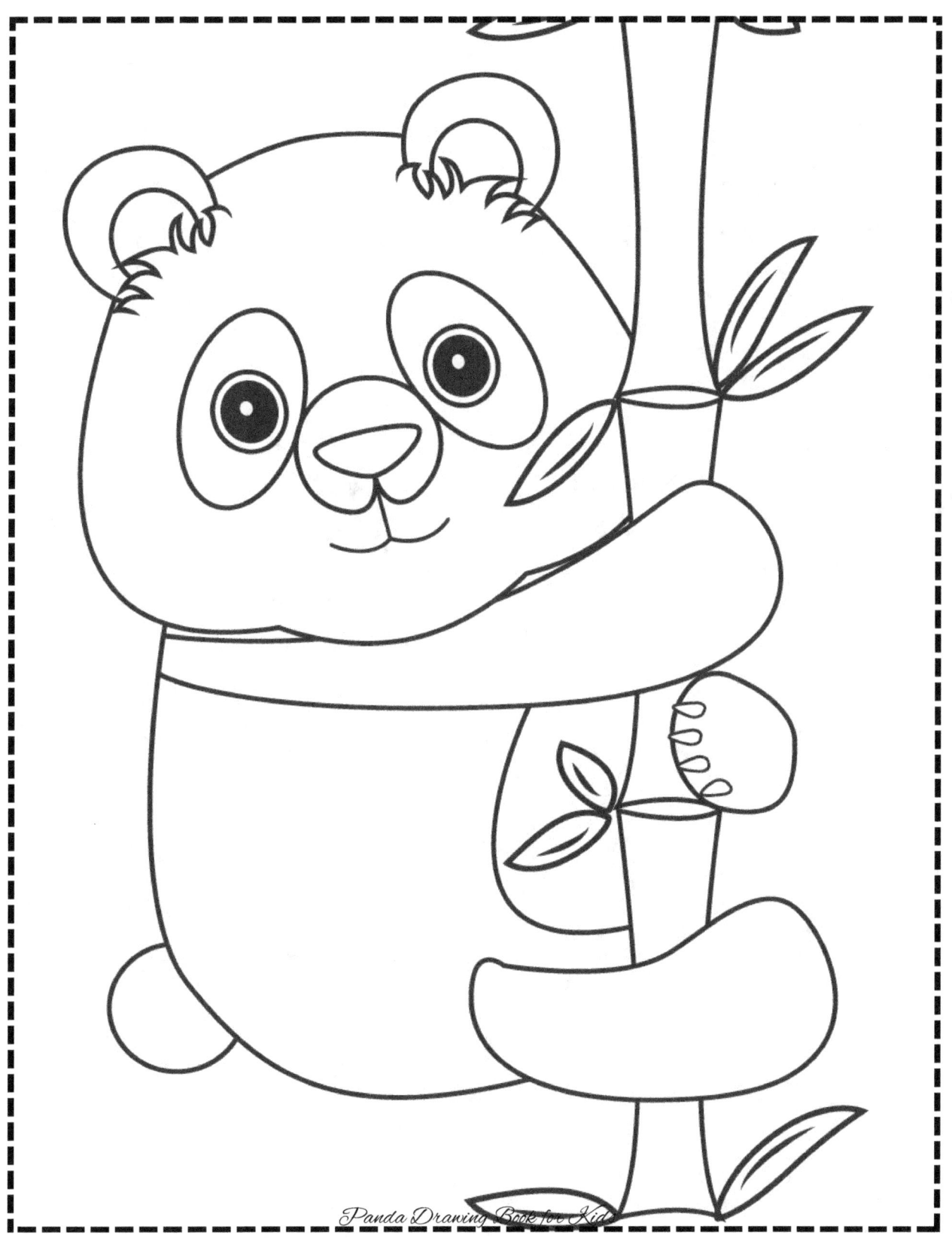

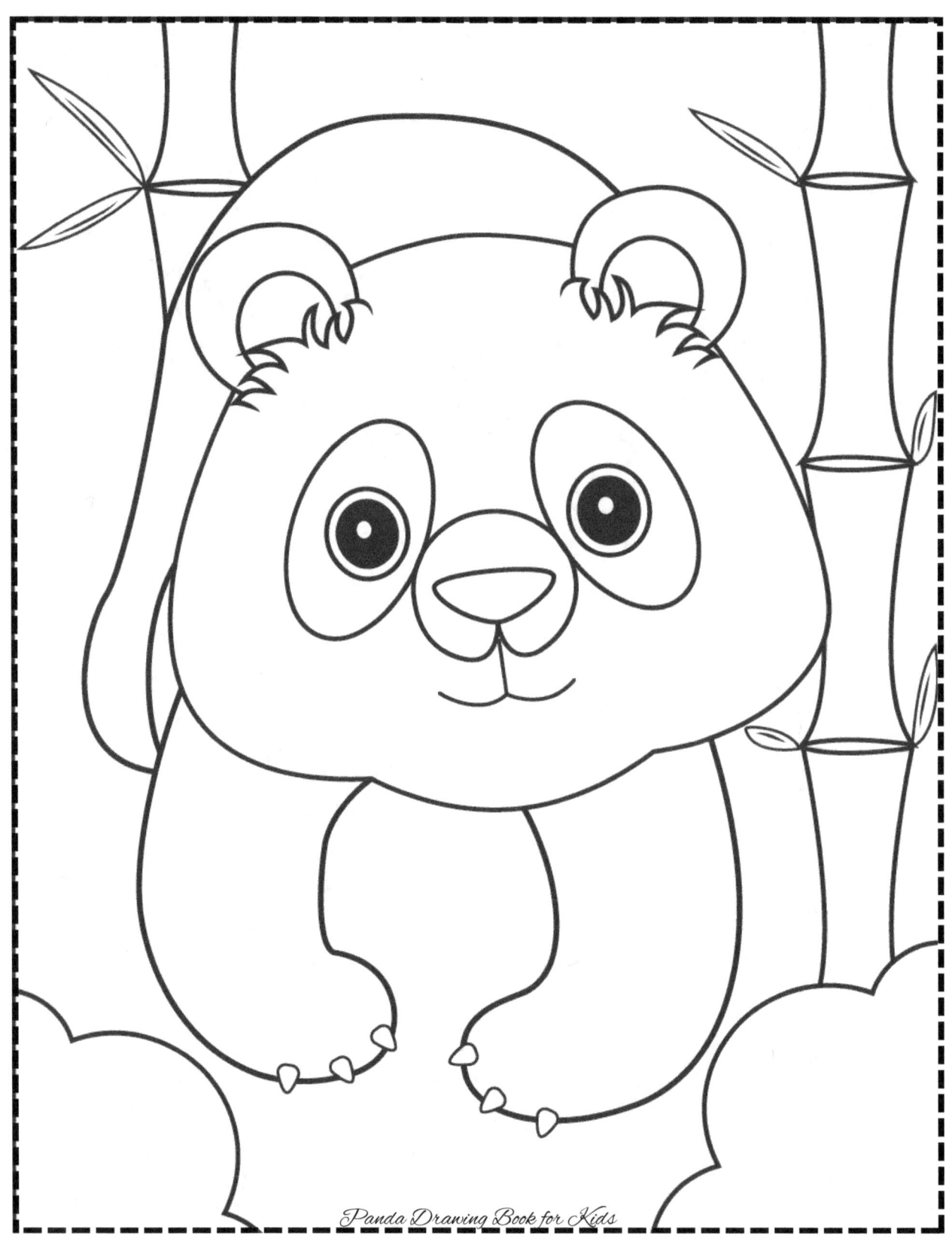

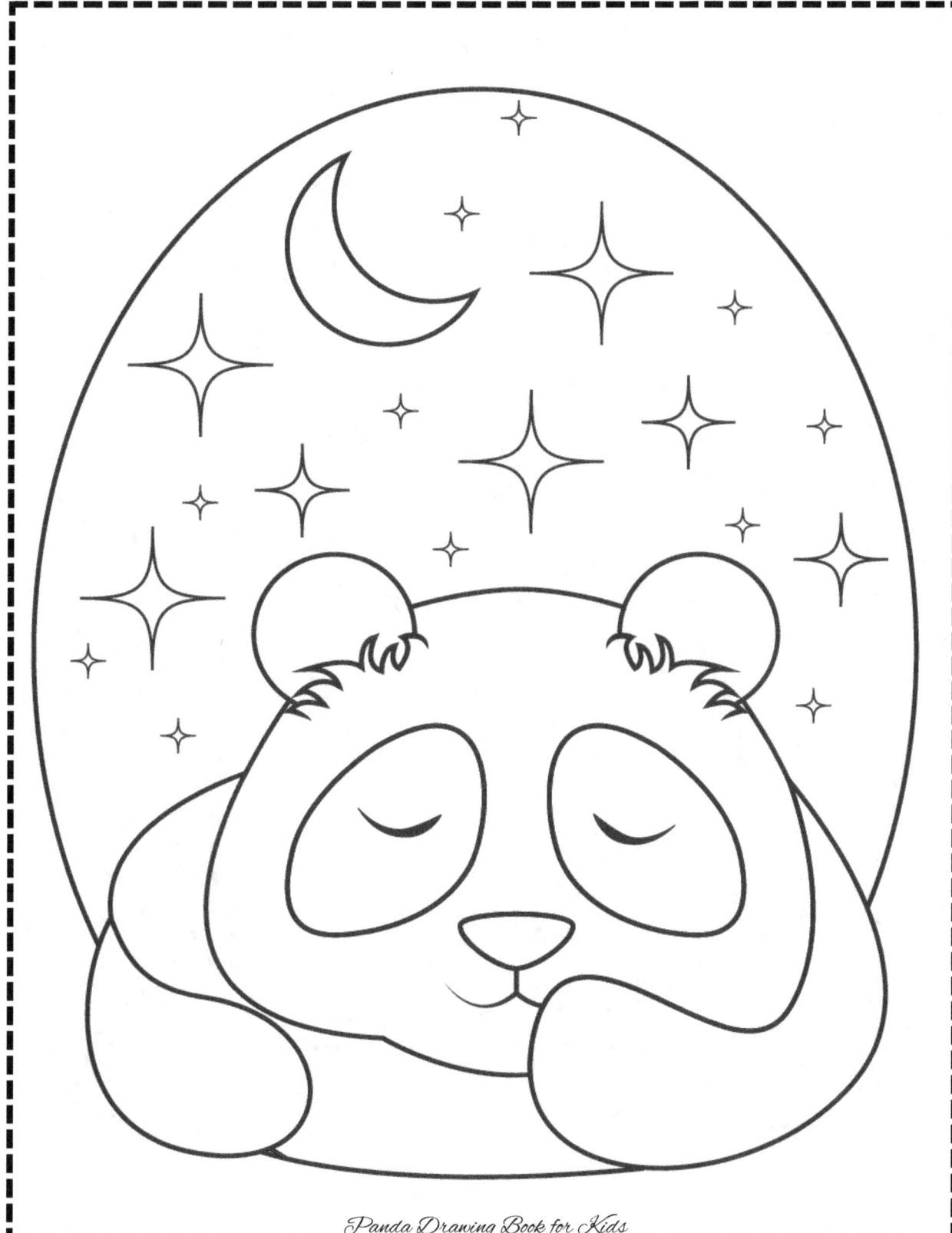

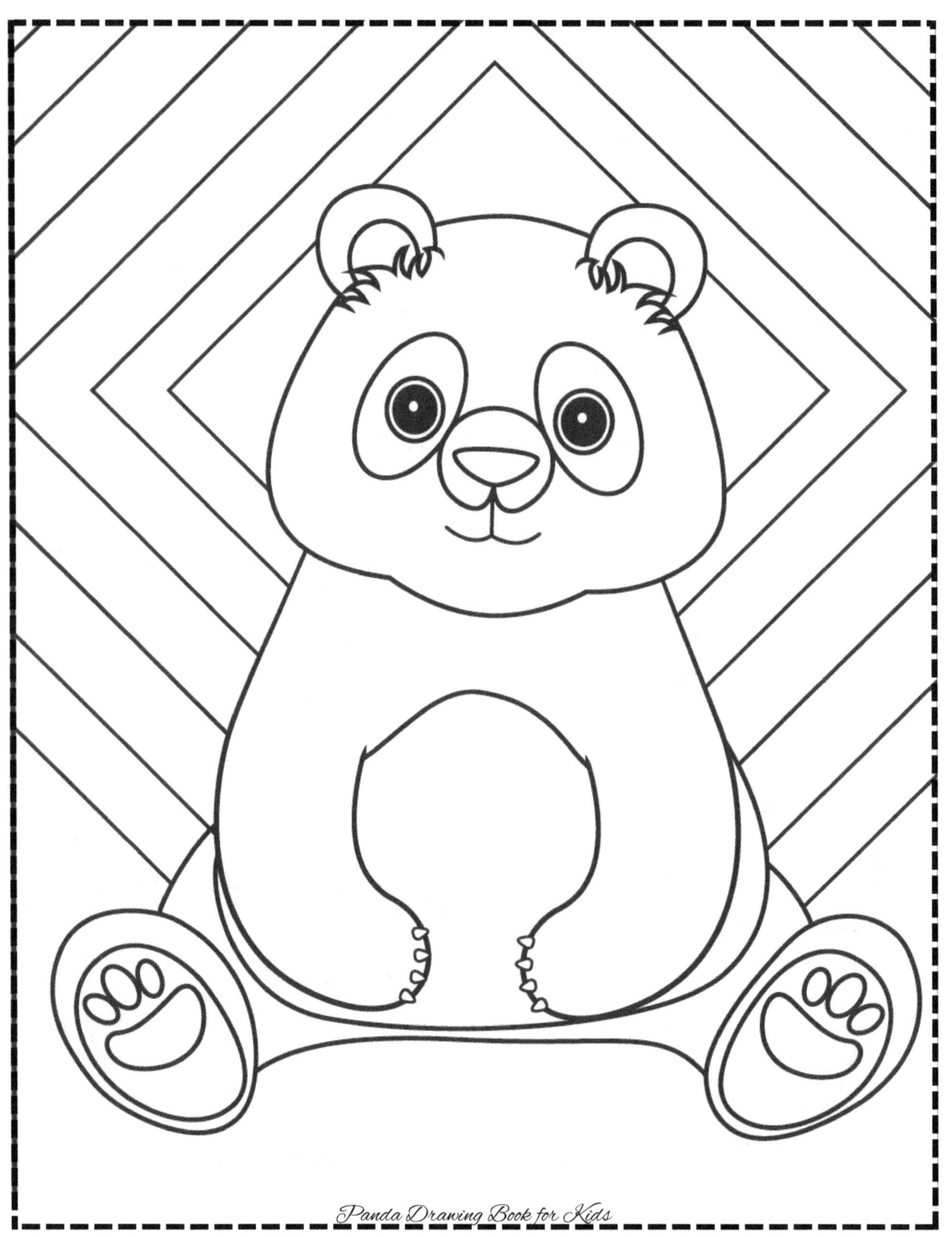

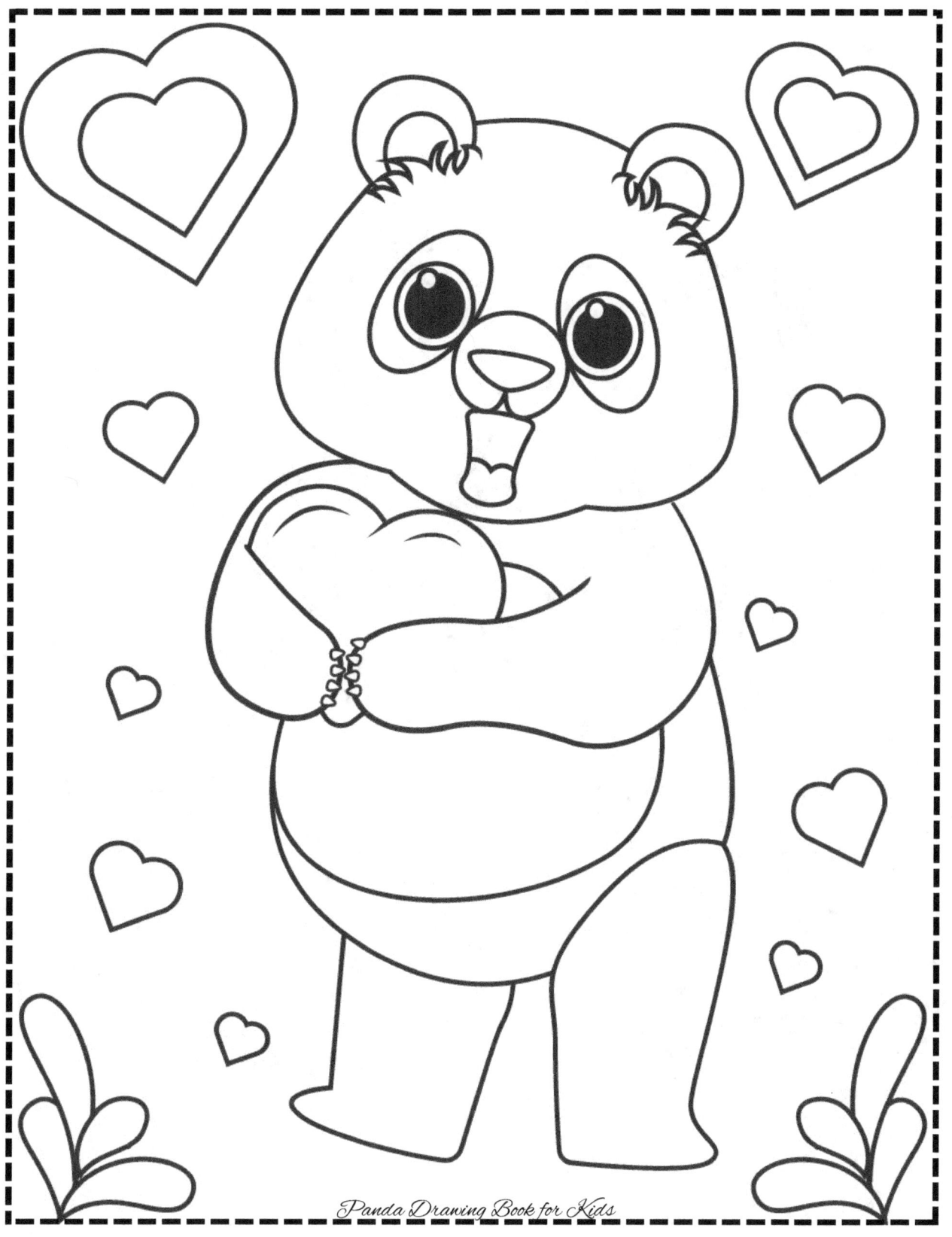

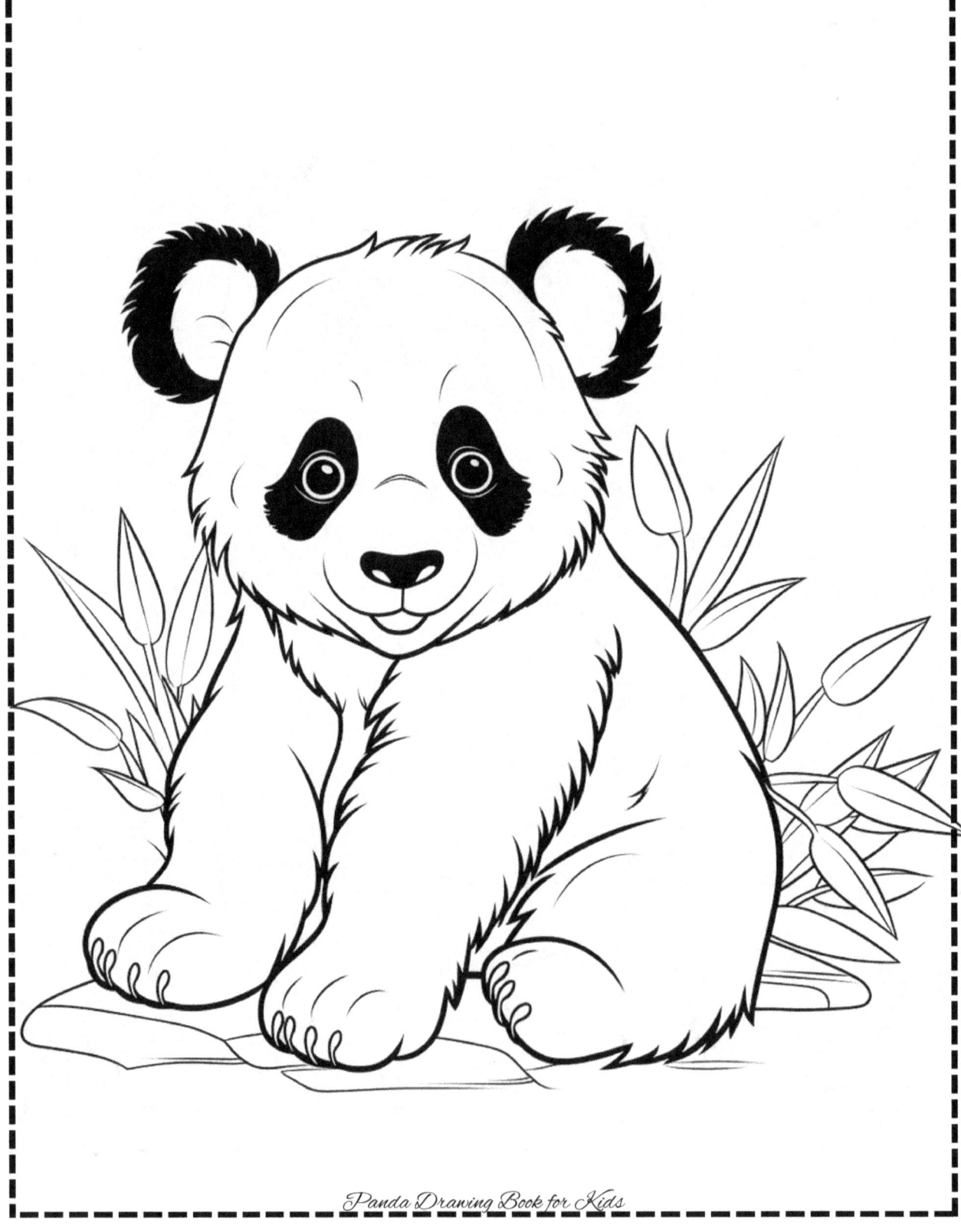

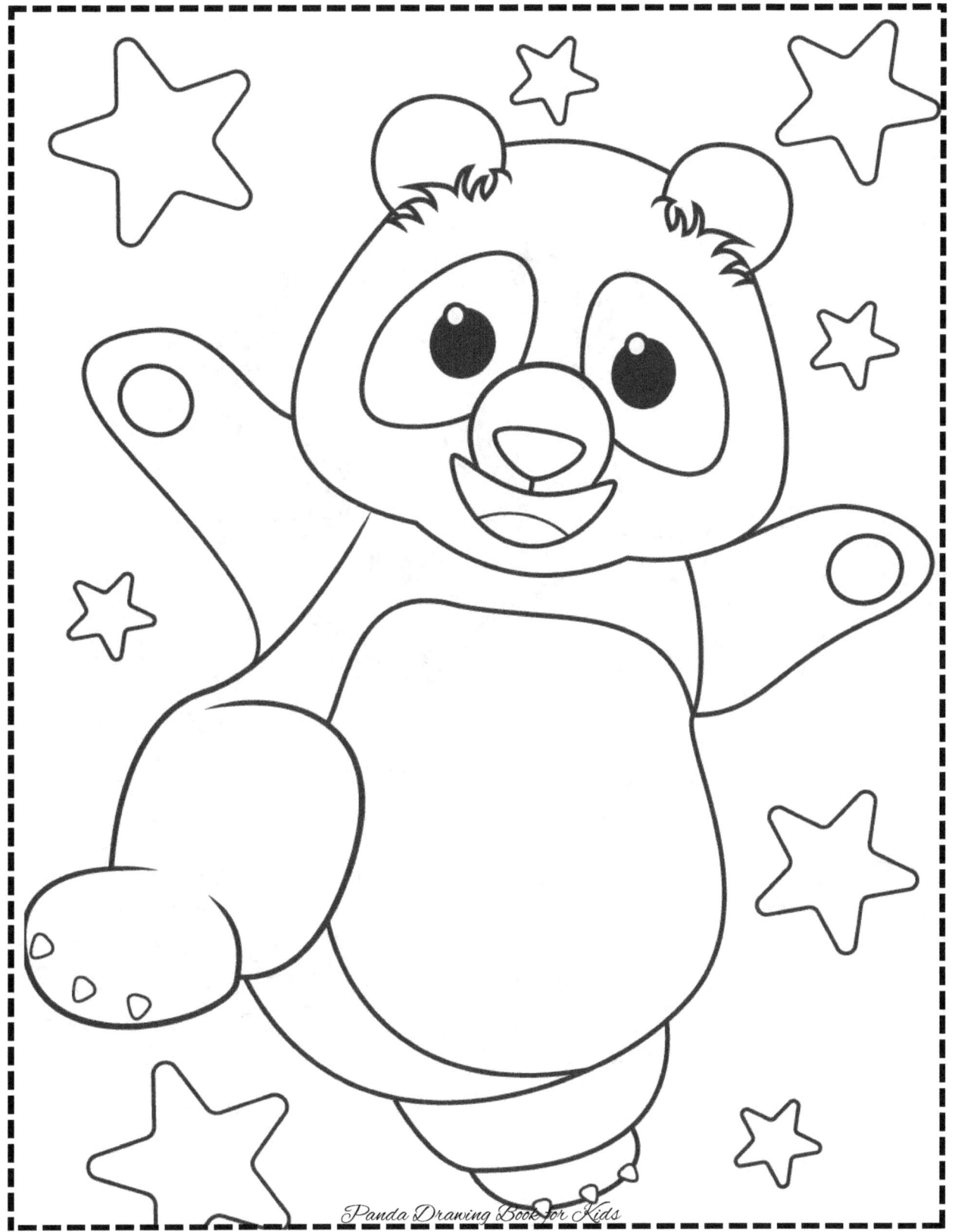

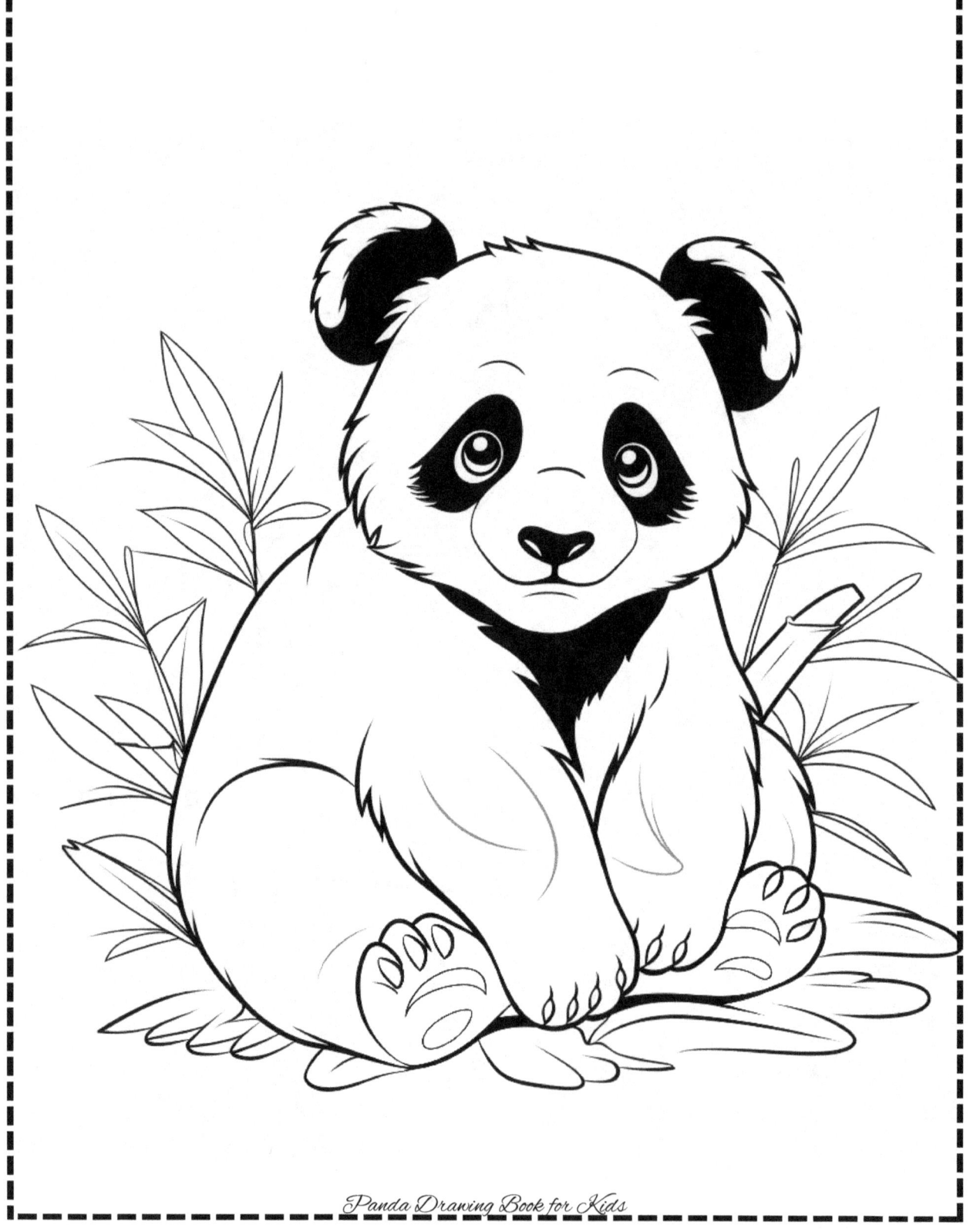

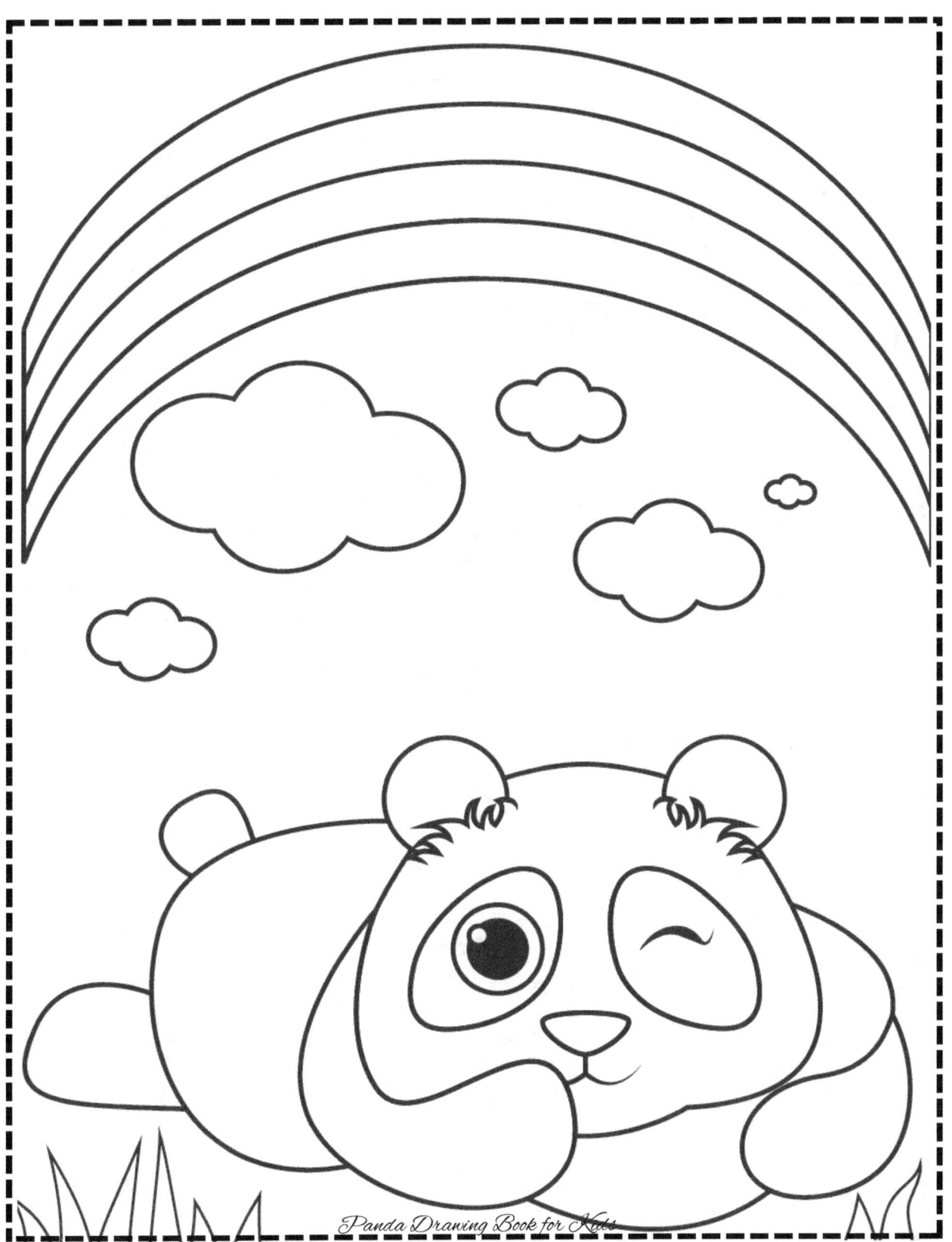

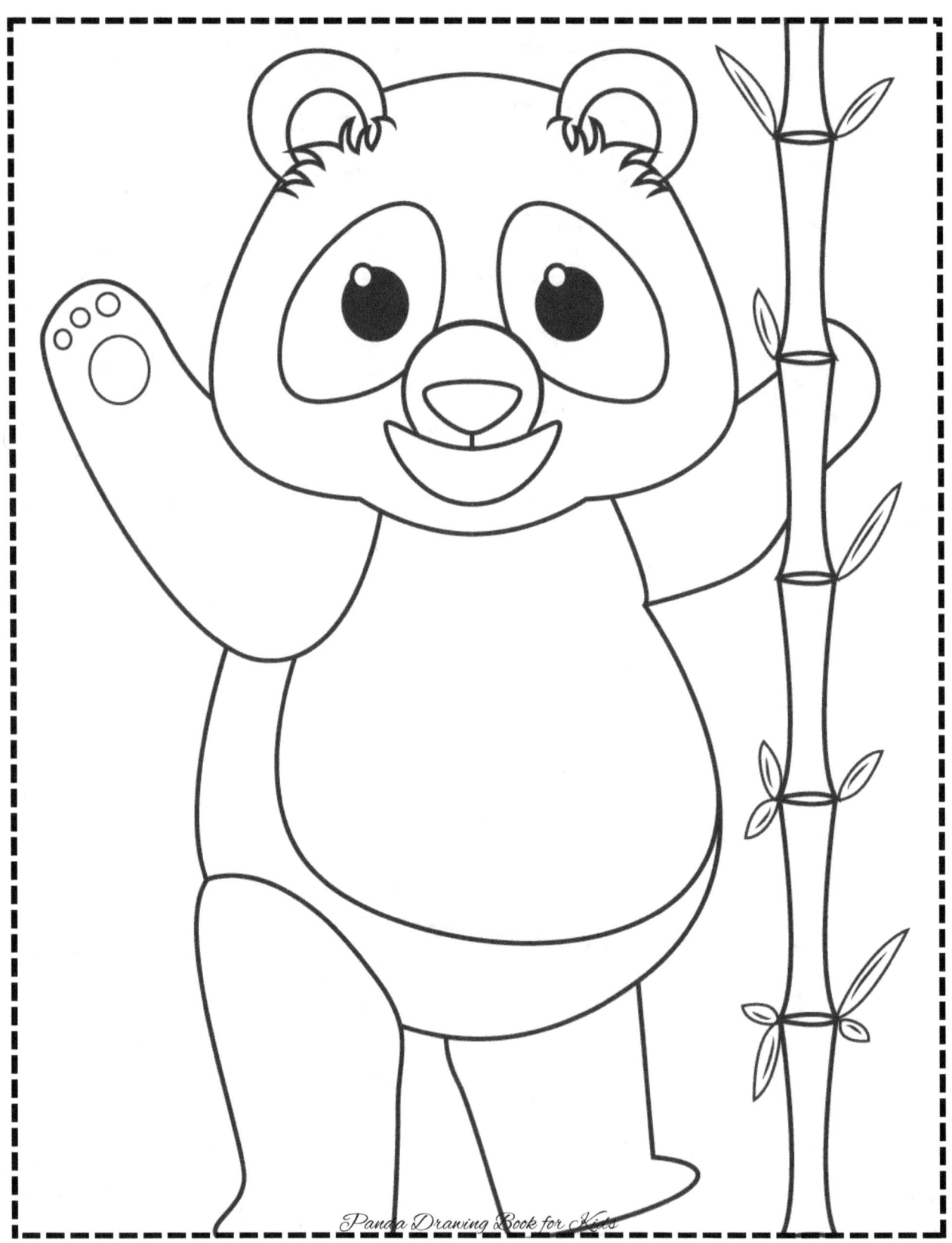

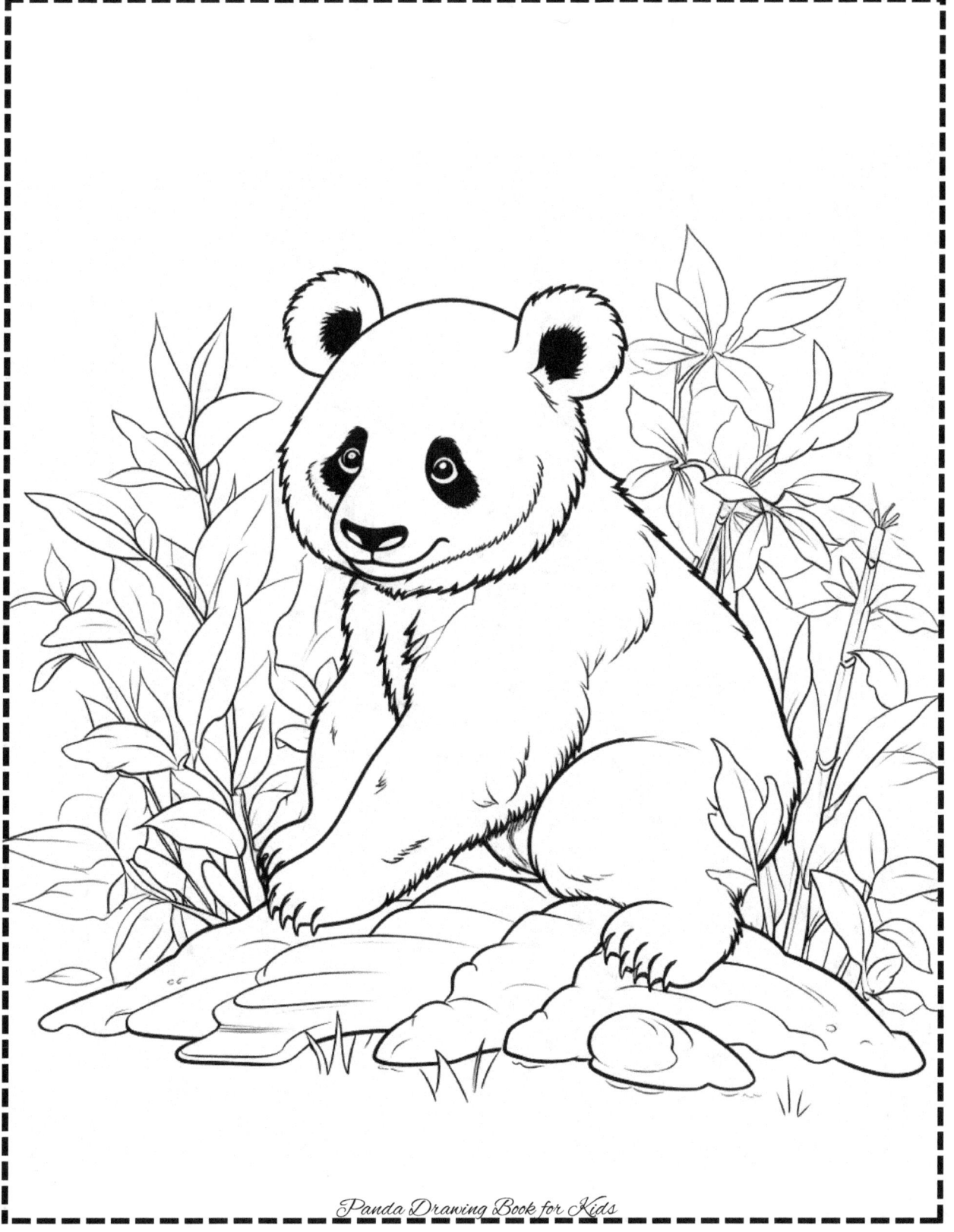

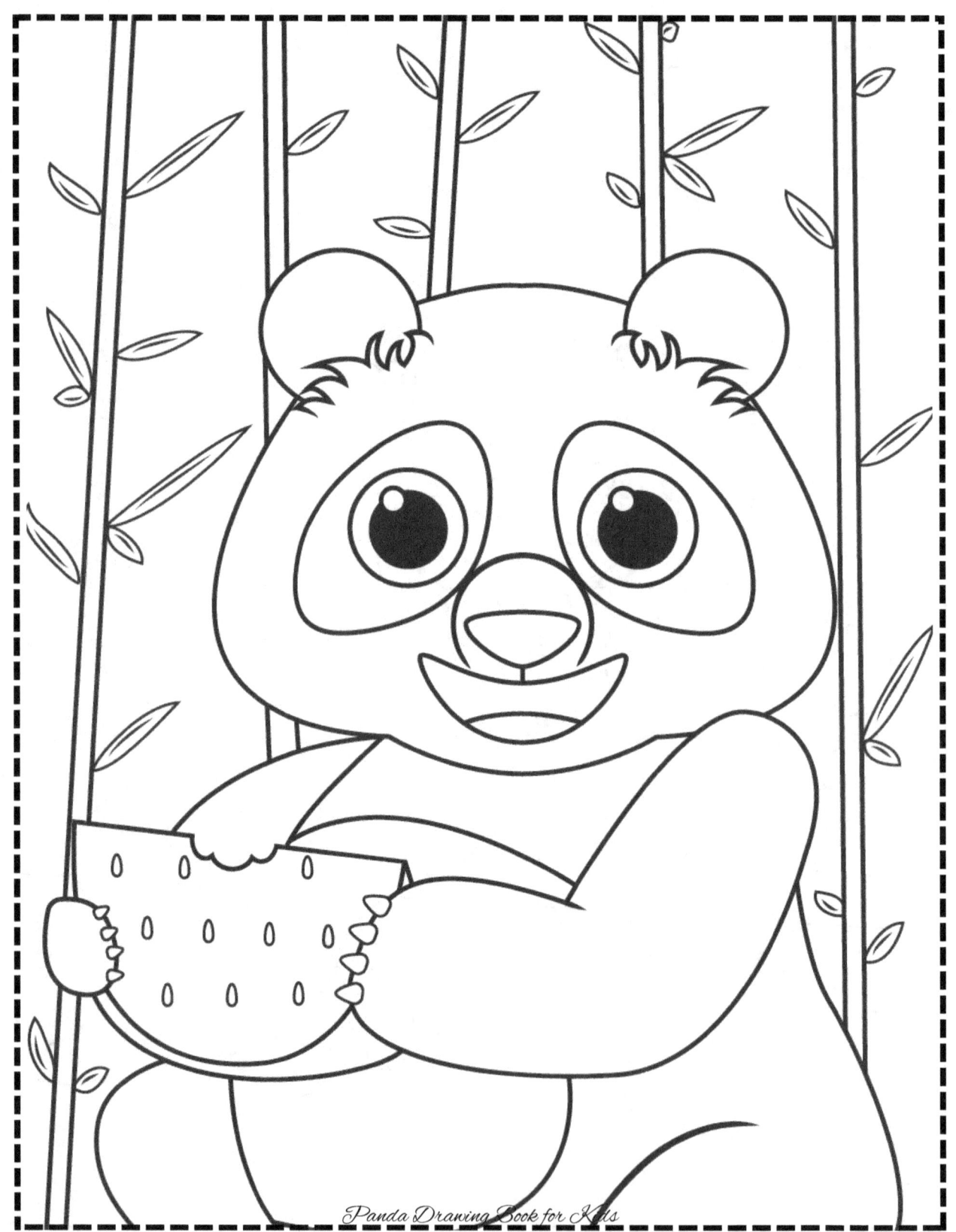

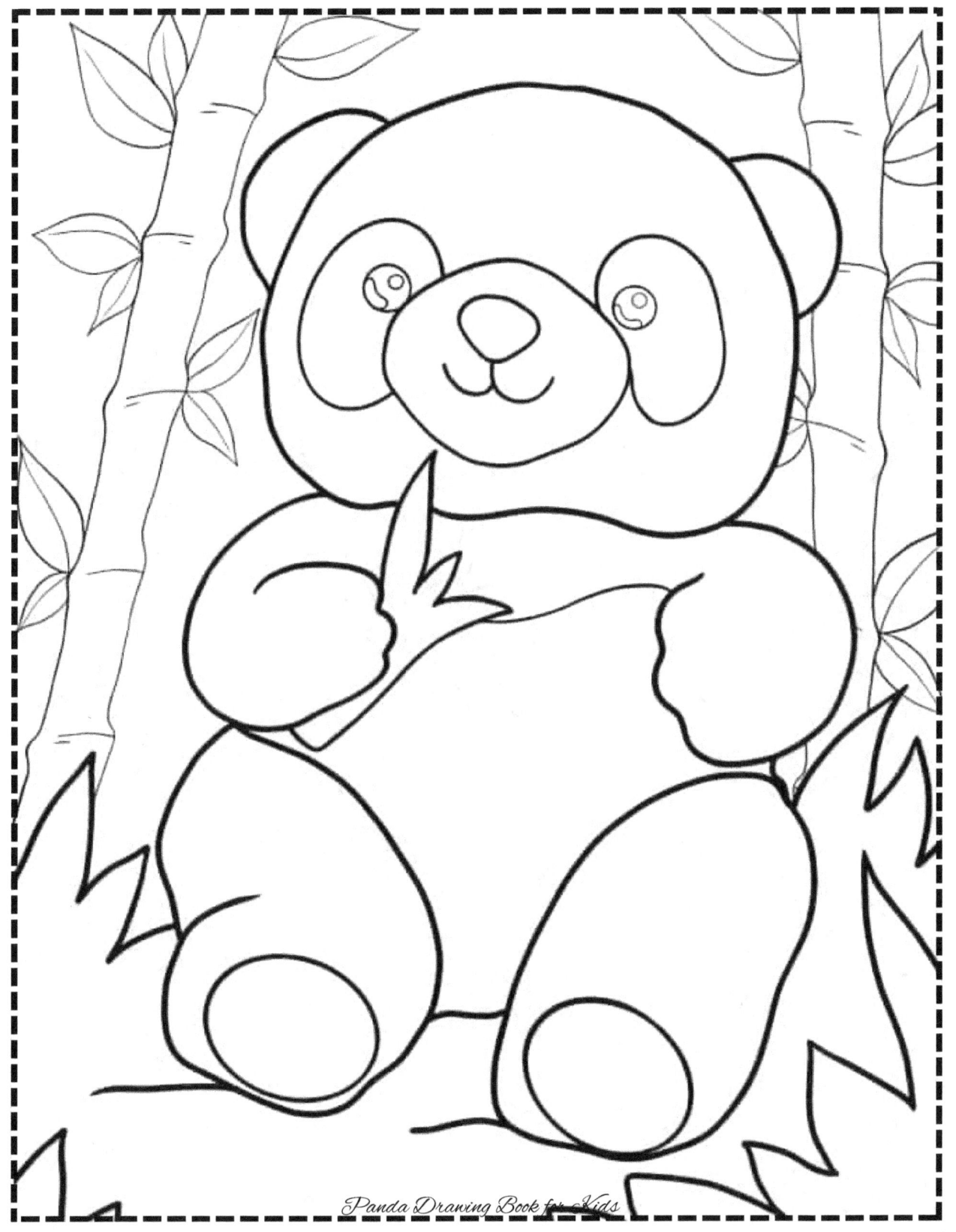

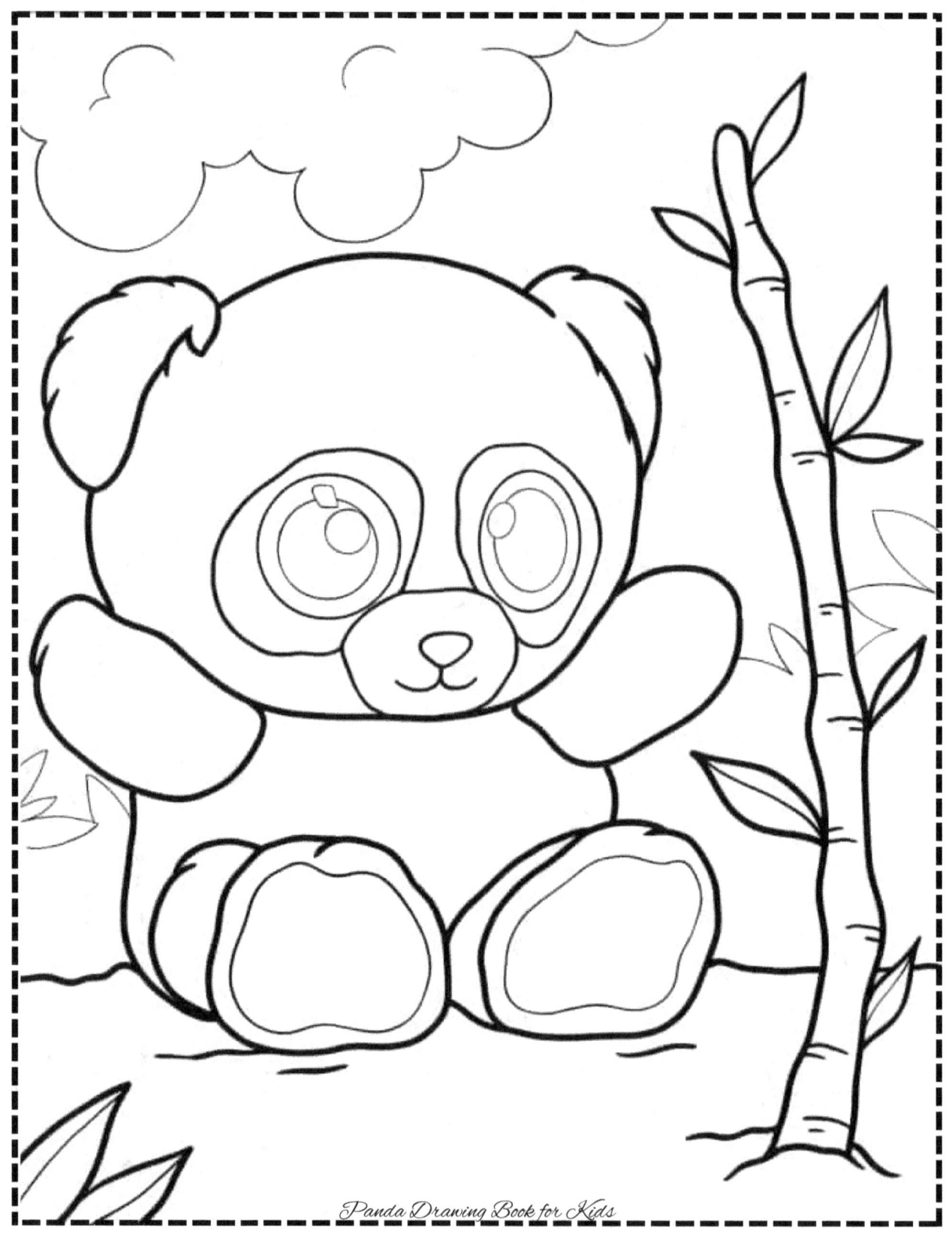

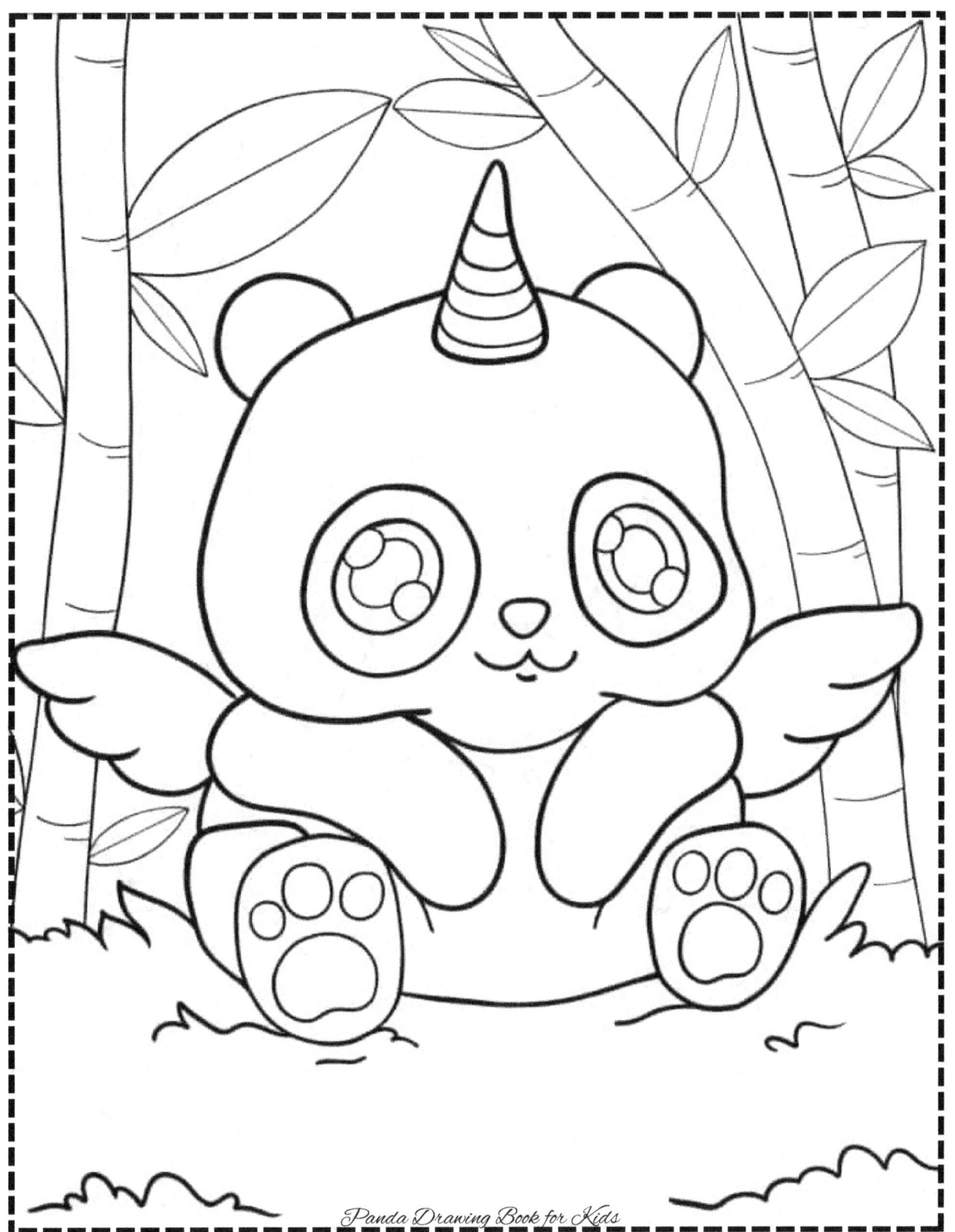

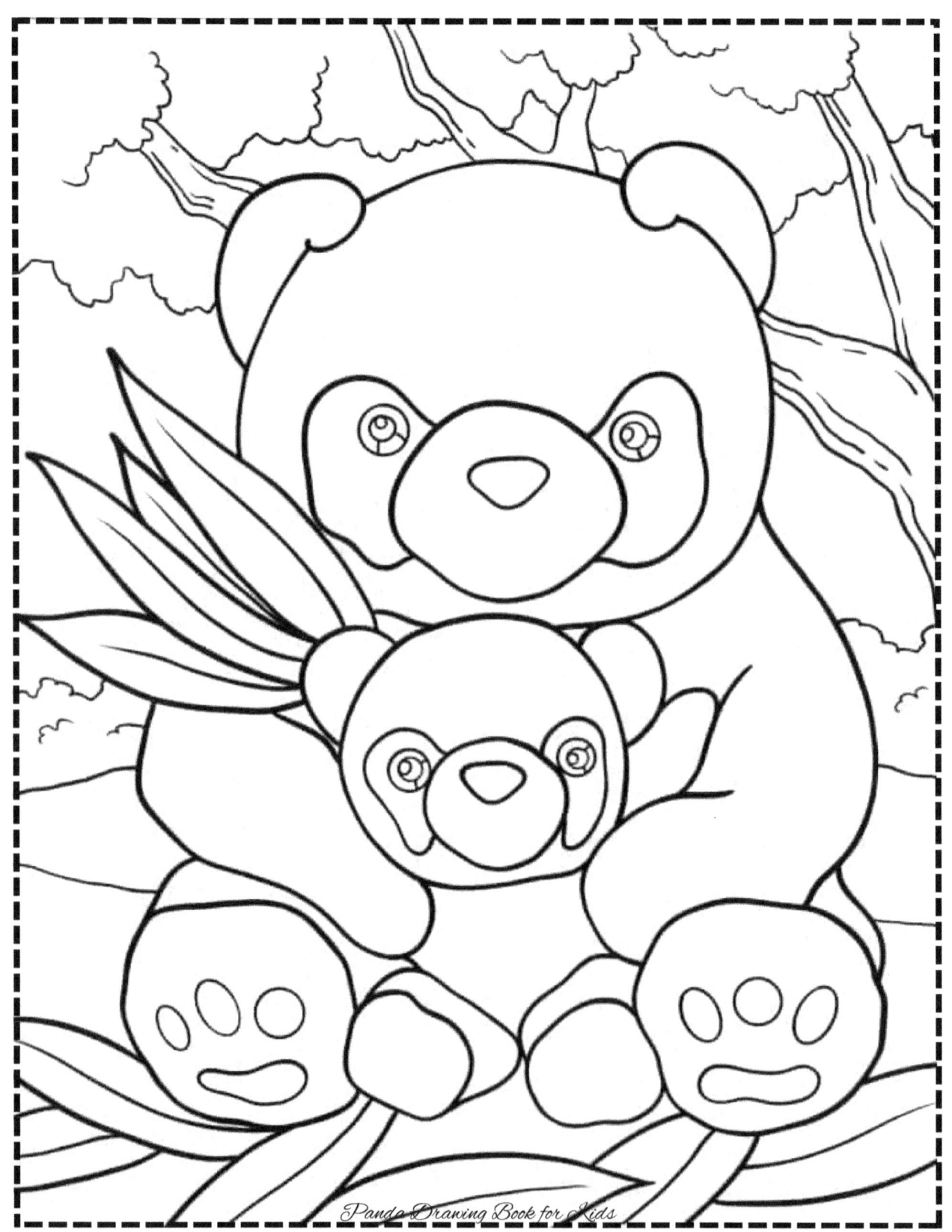

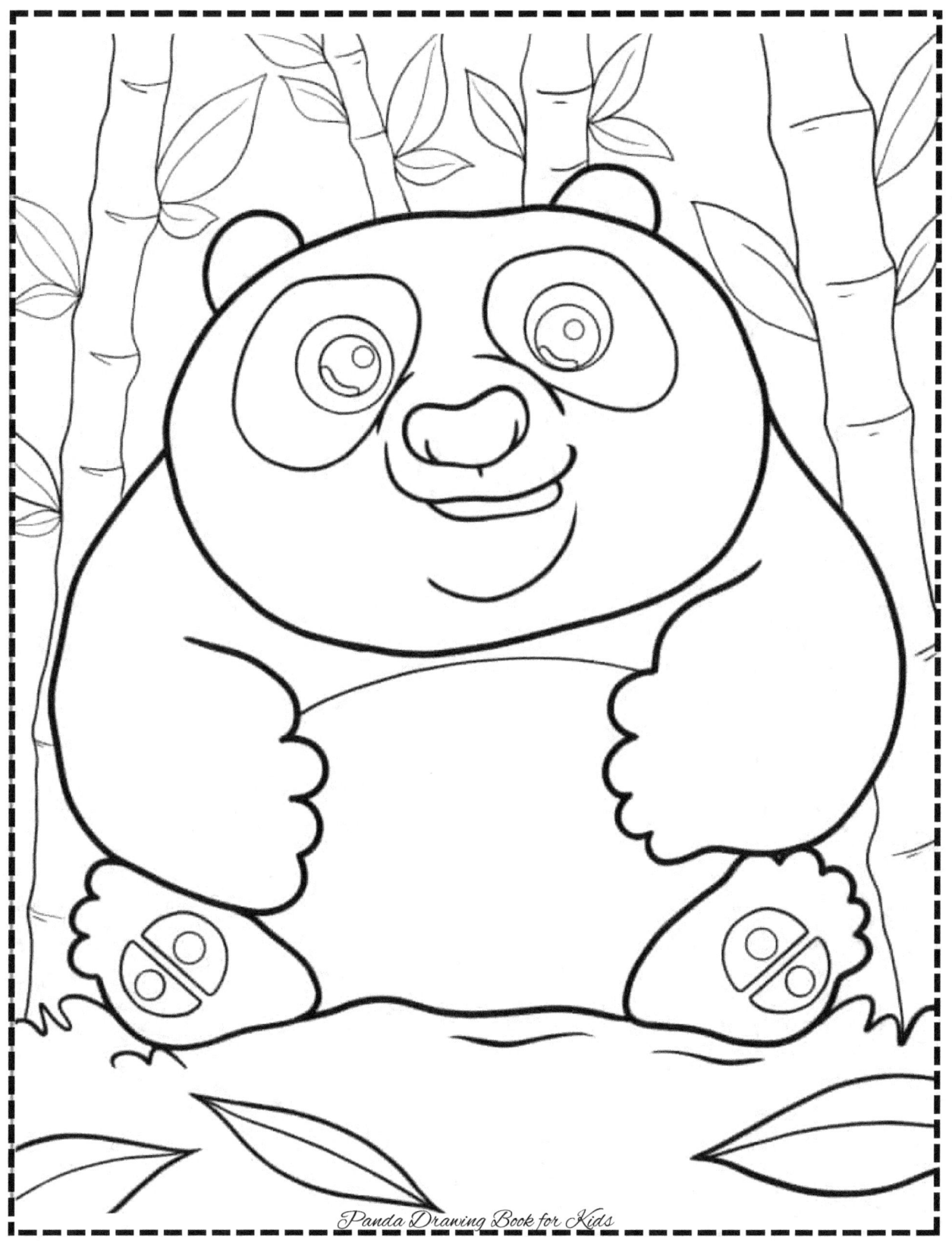

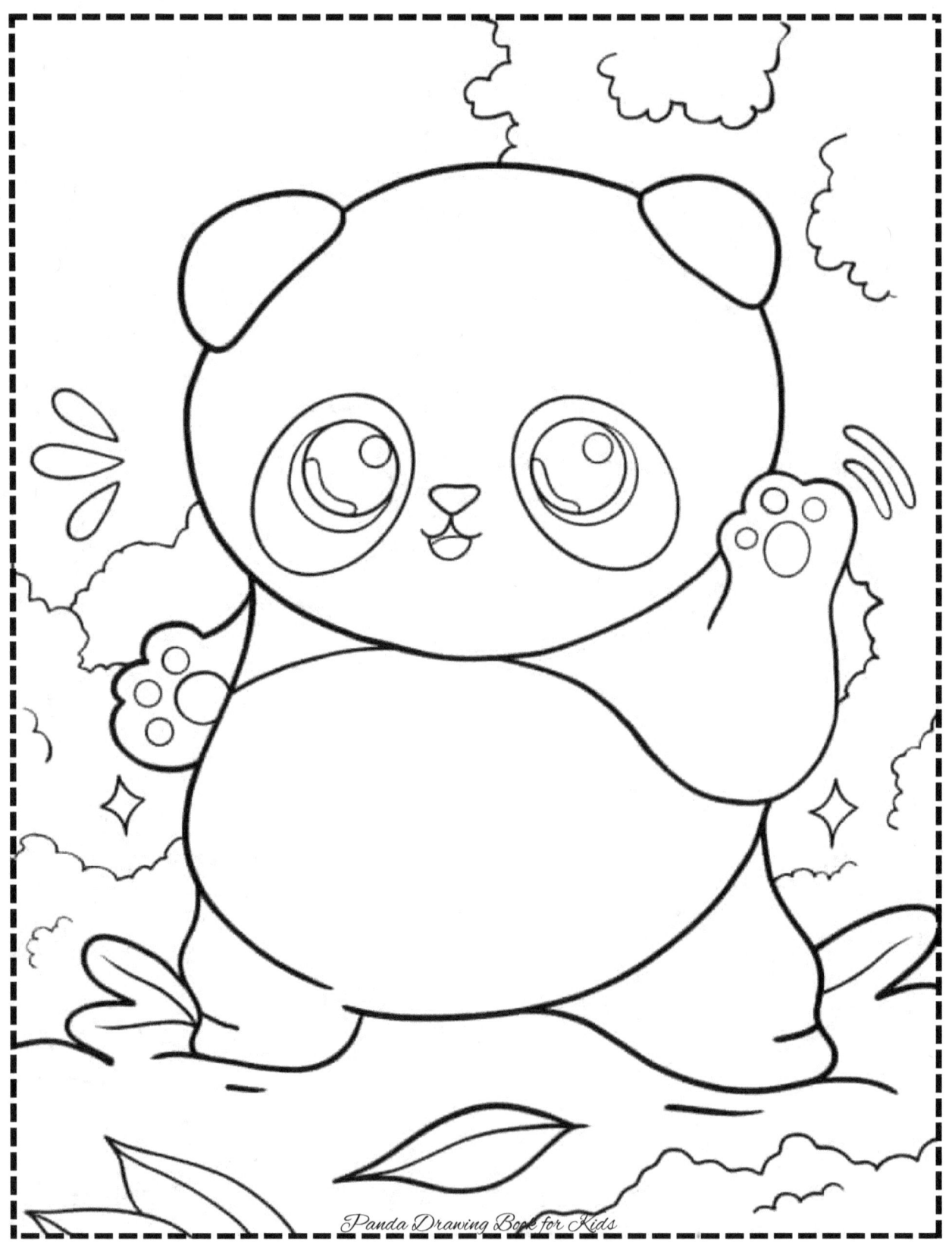

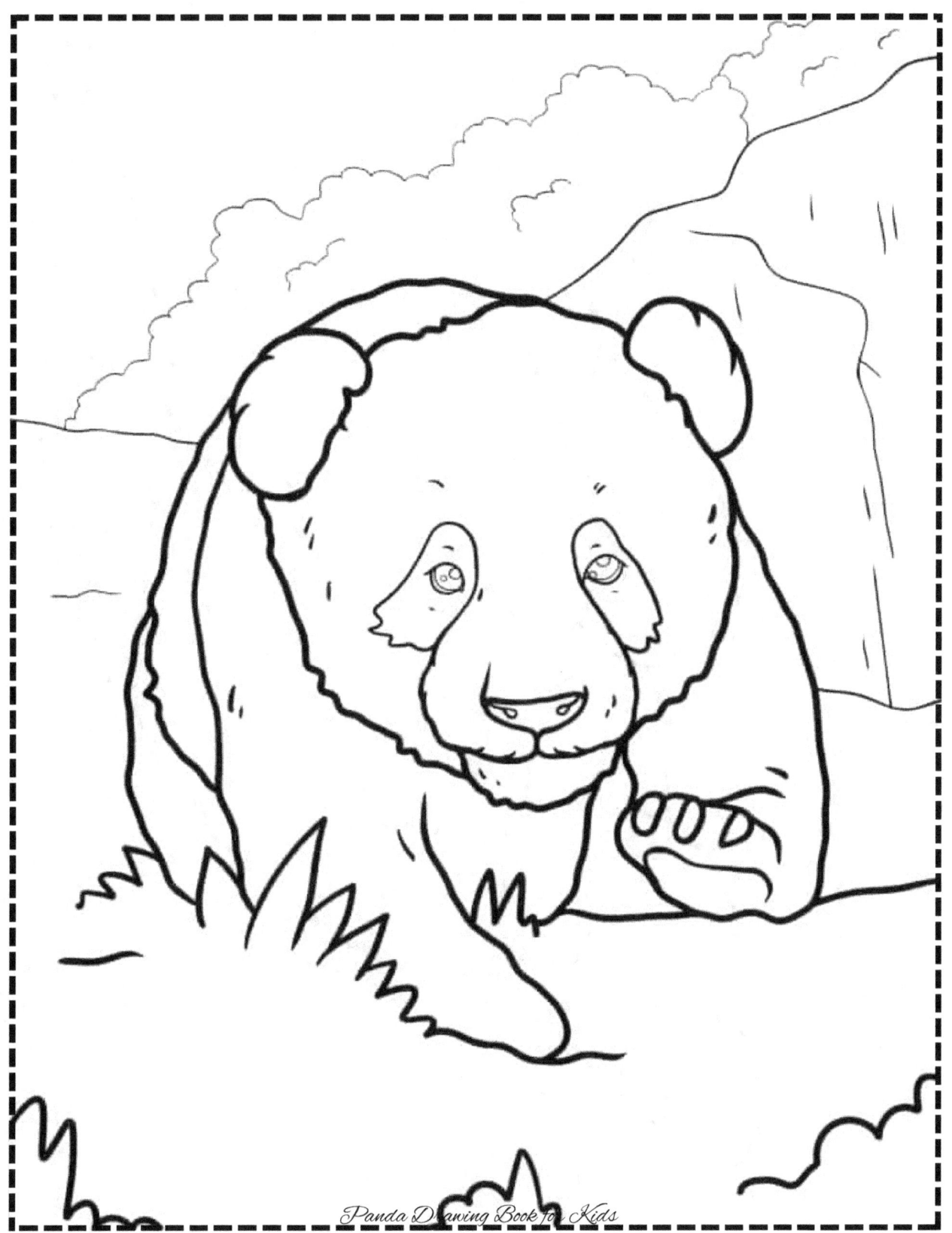

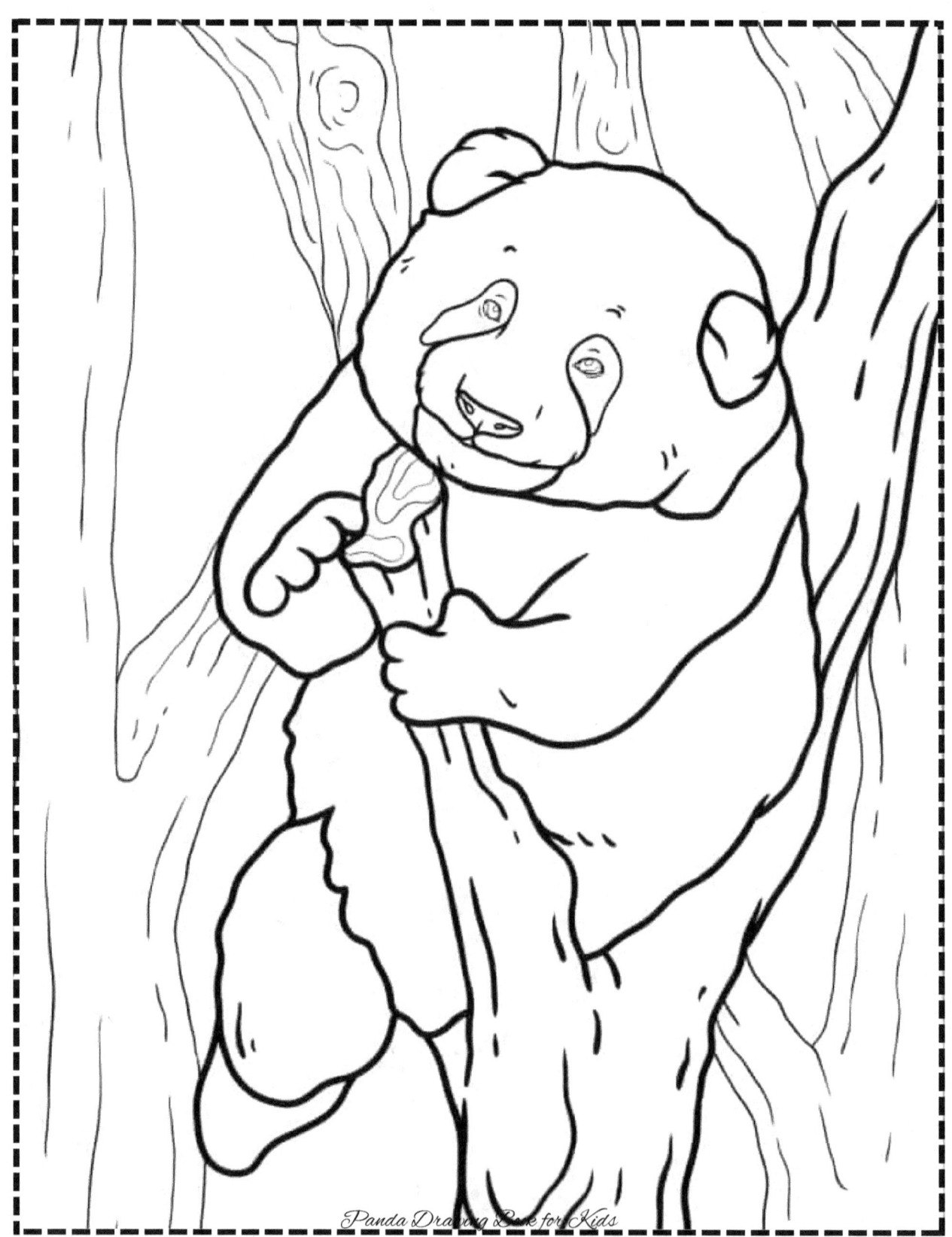

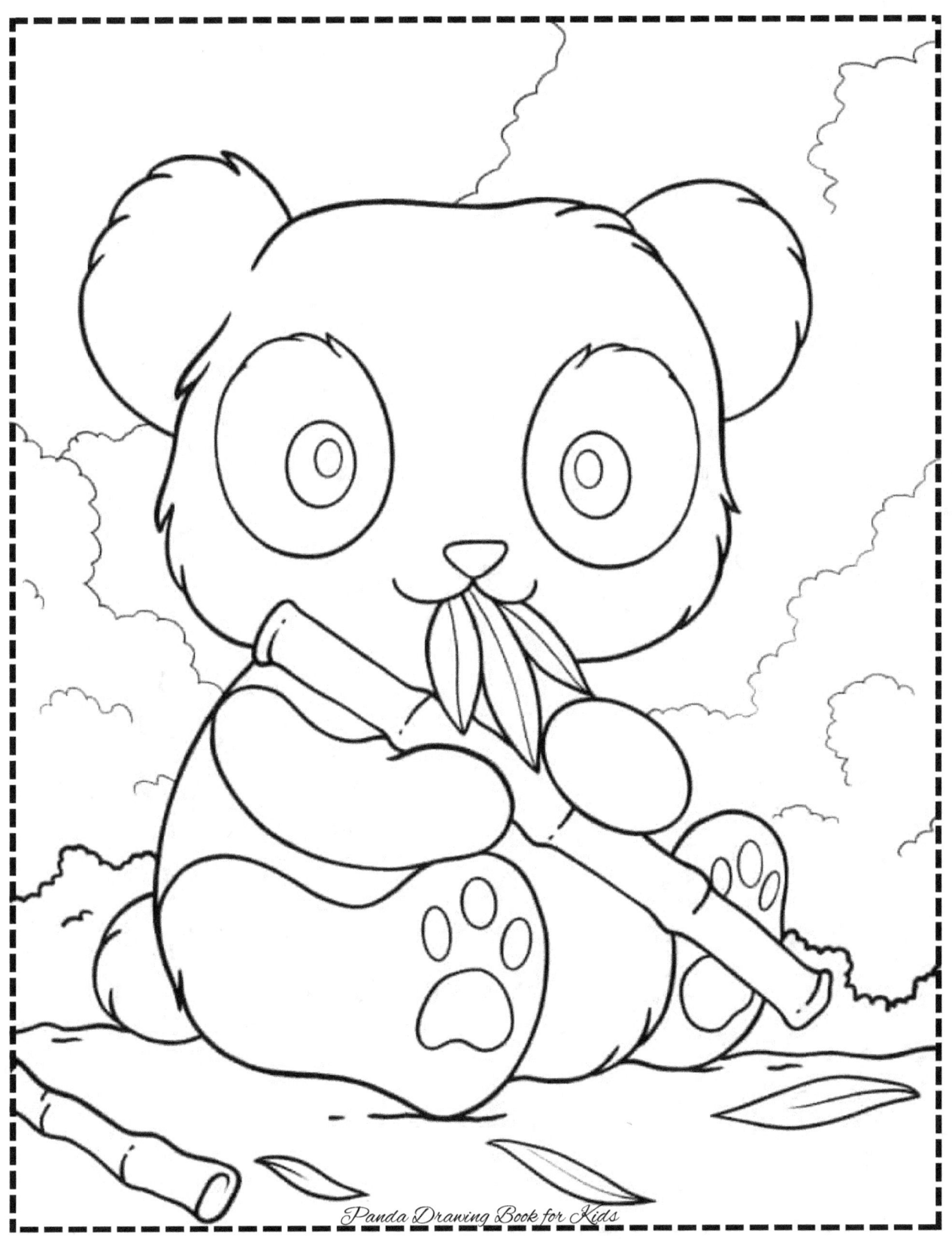

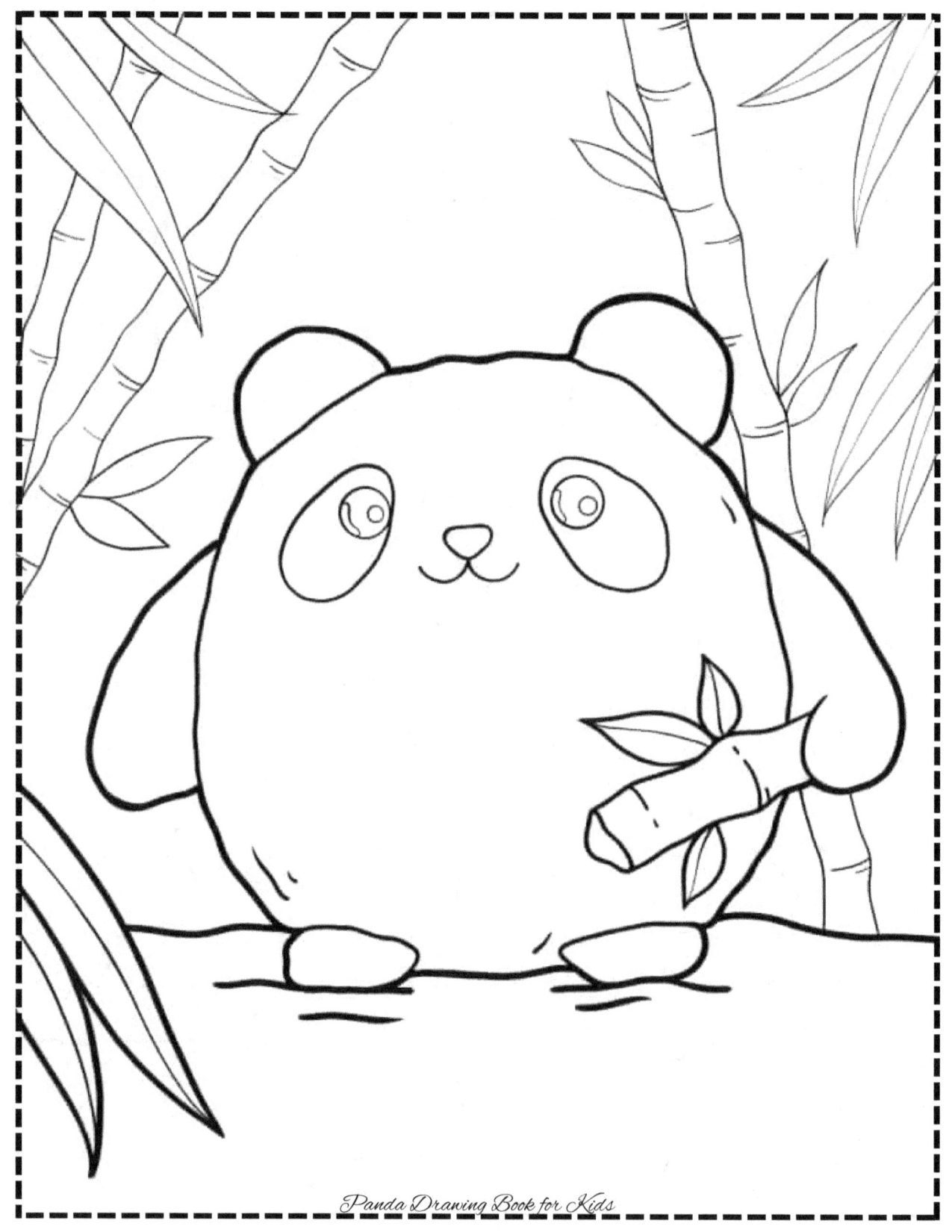

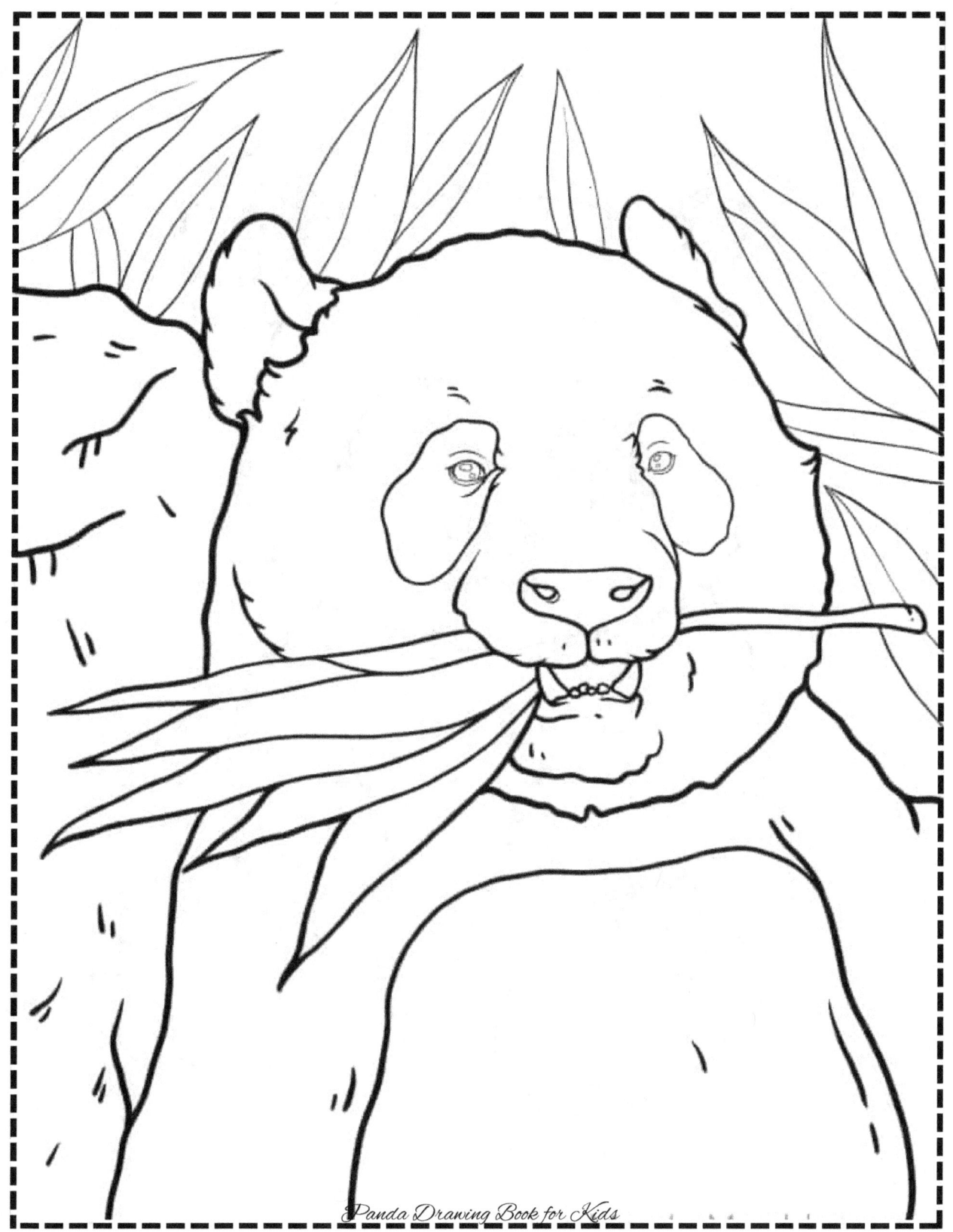

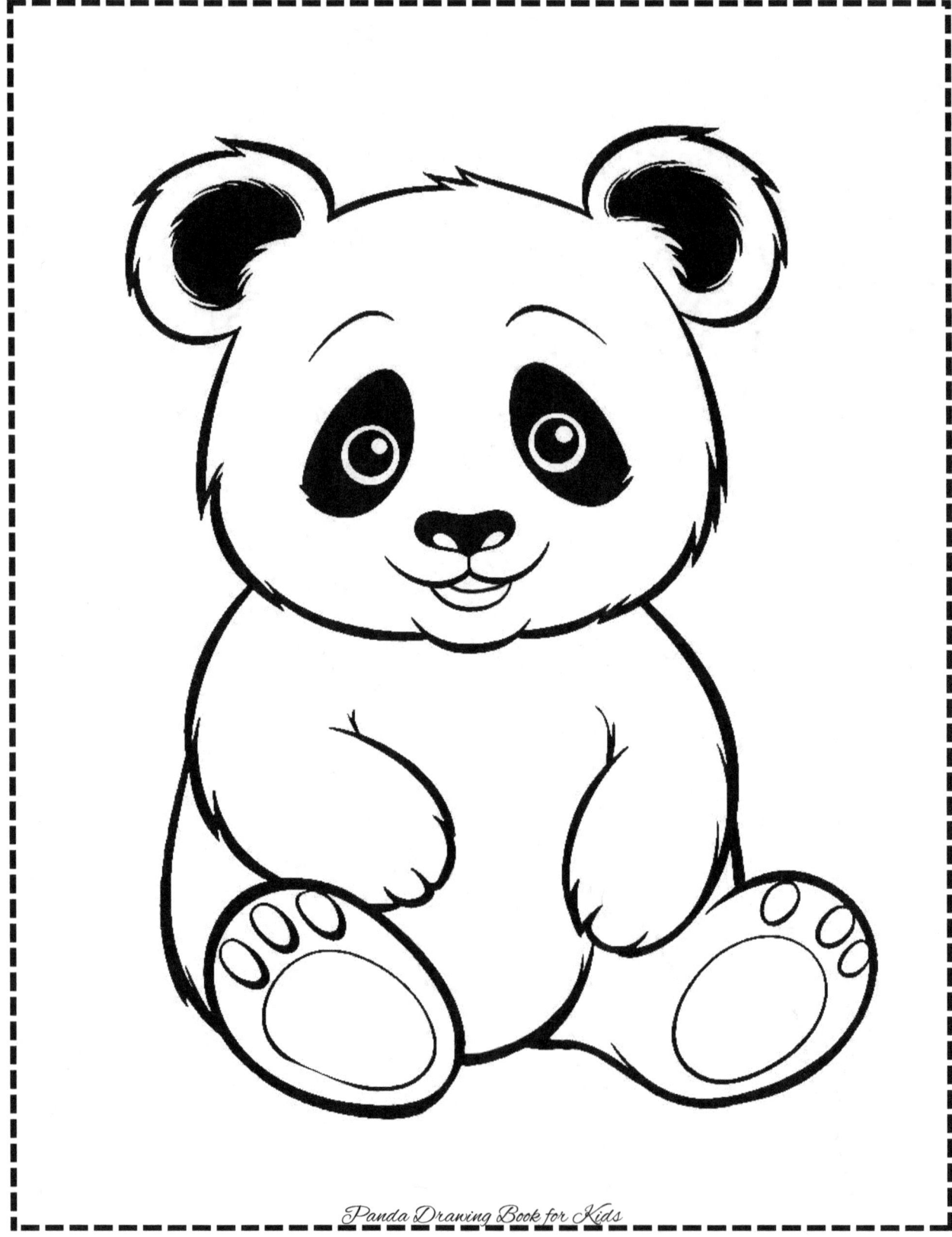

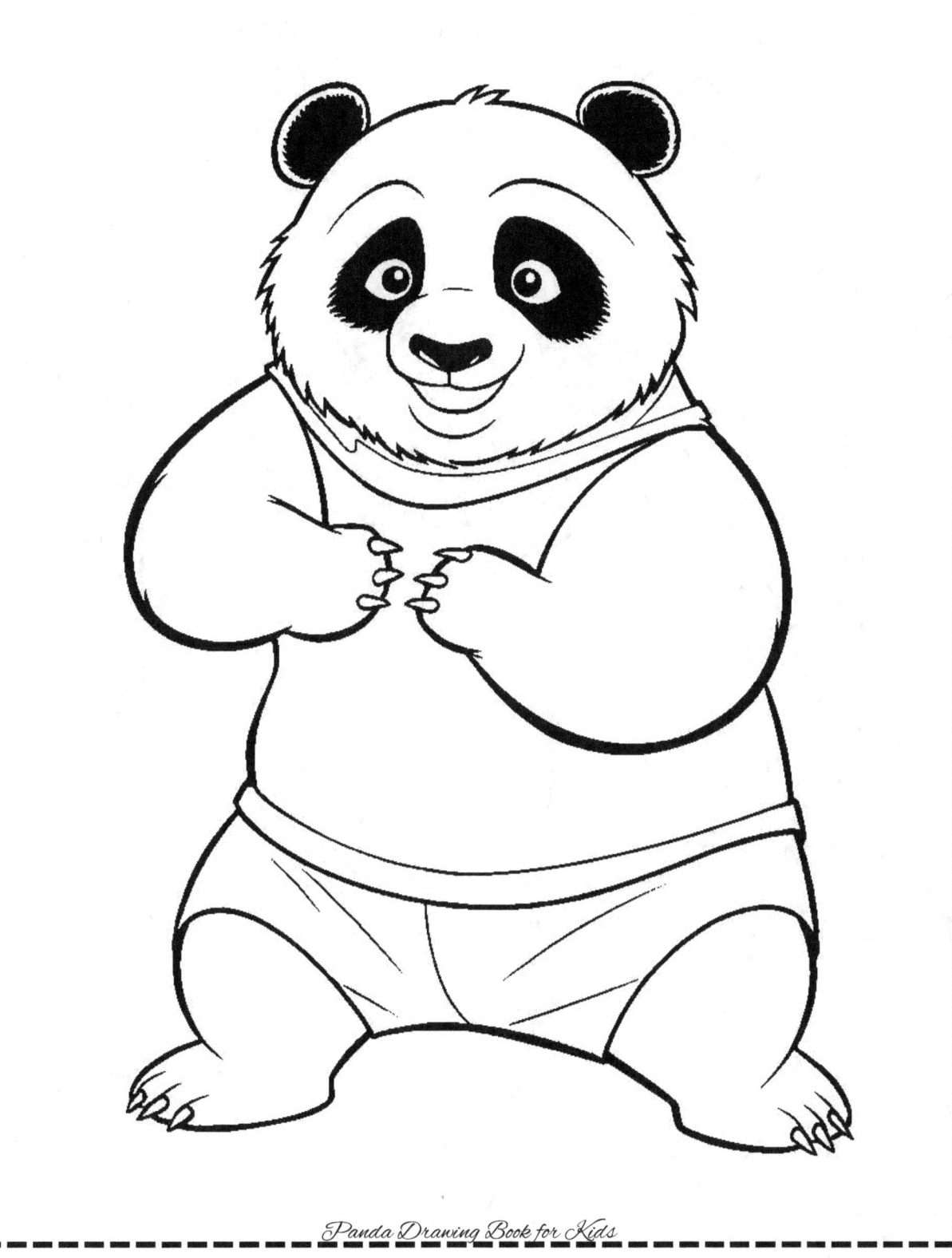

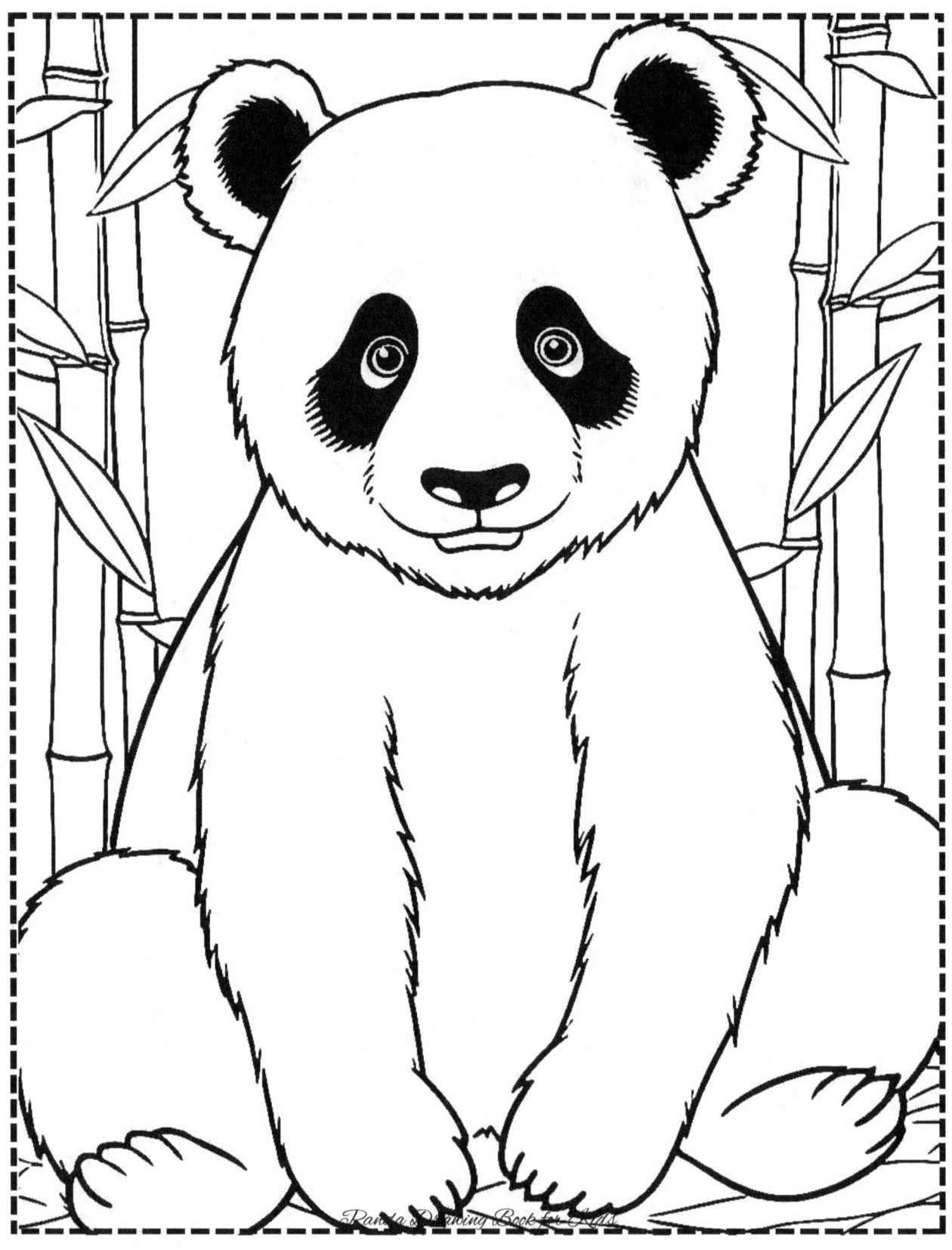

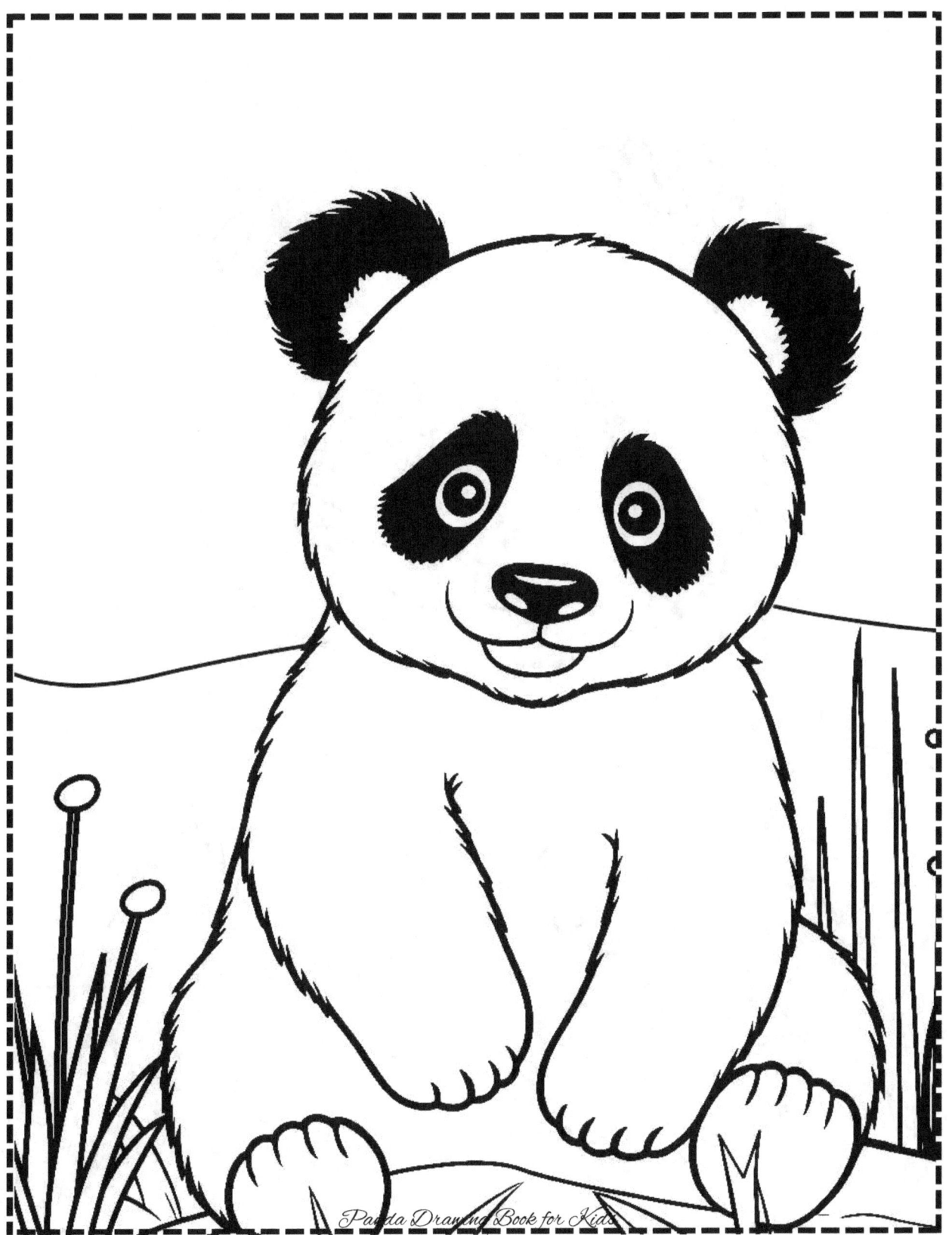

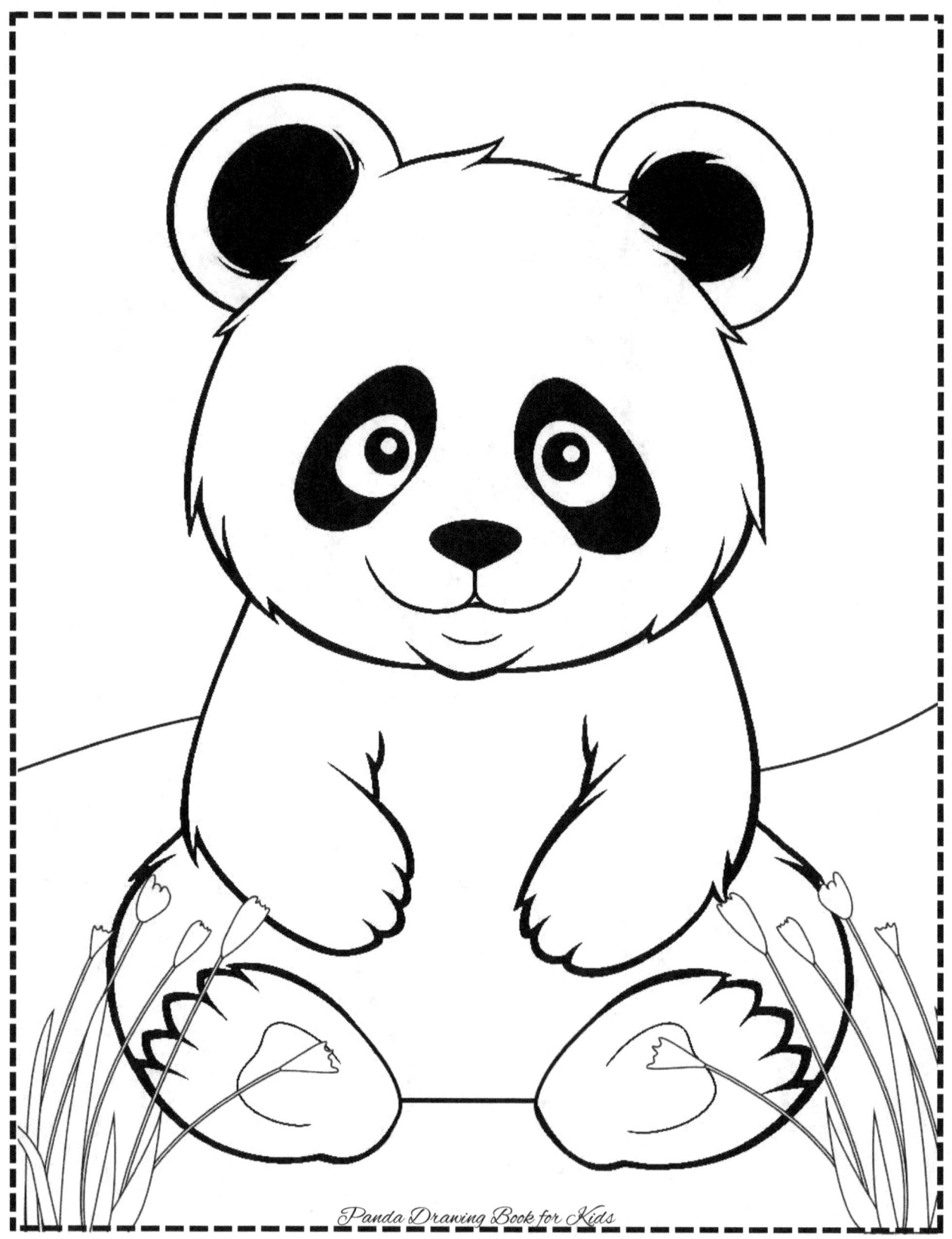

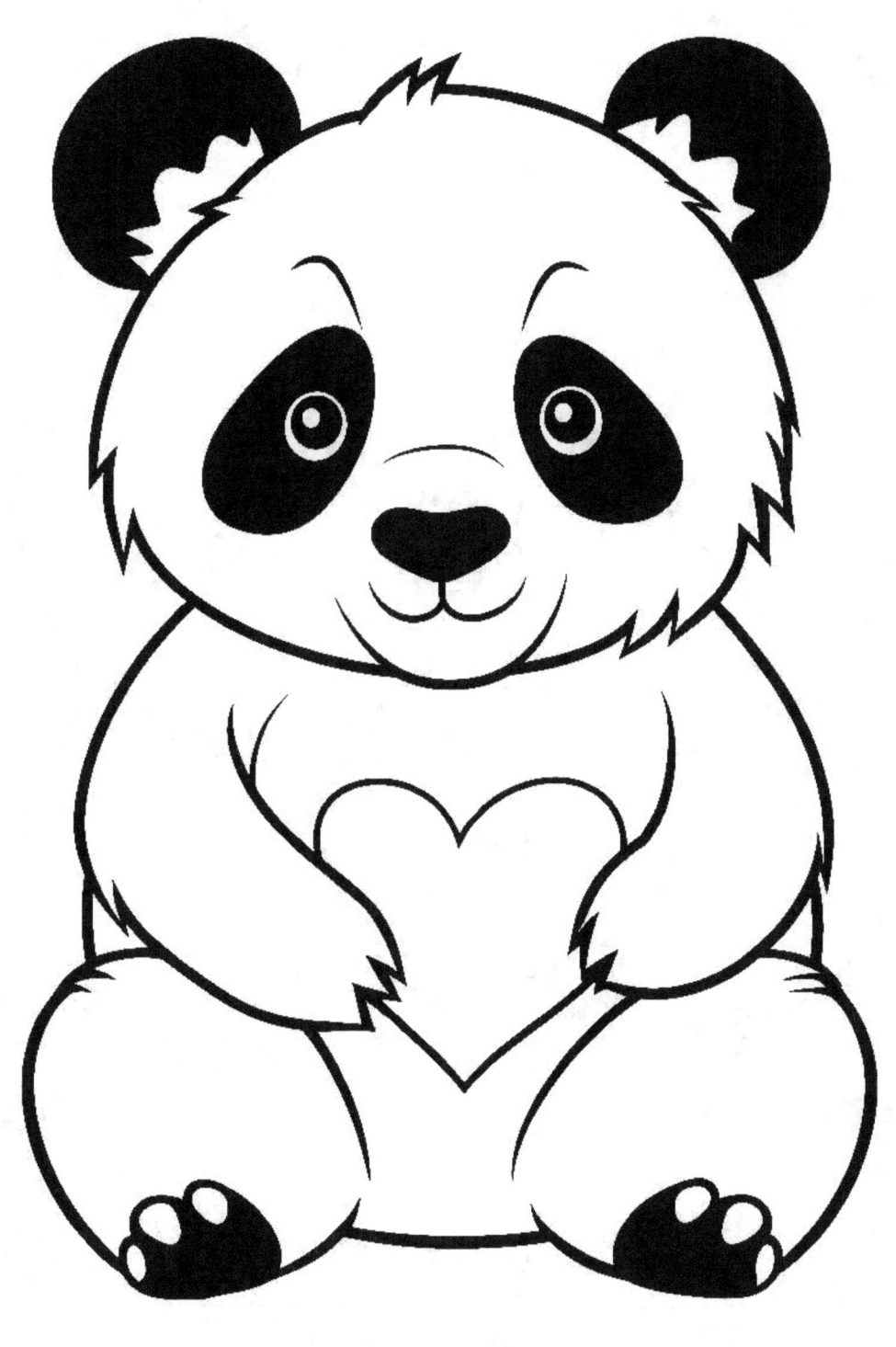

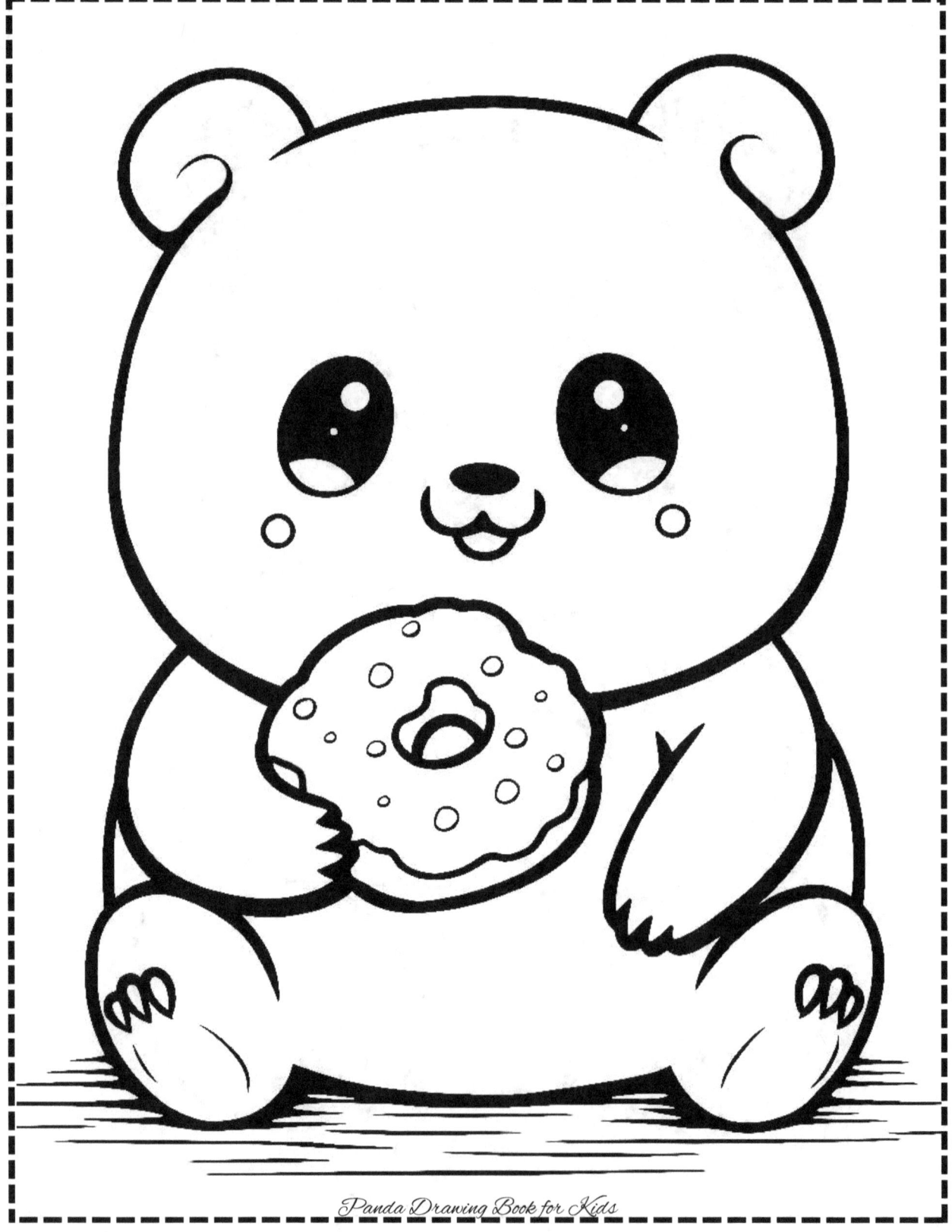

Panda Drawing Book for Kids

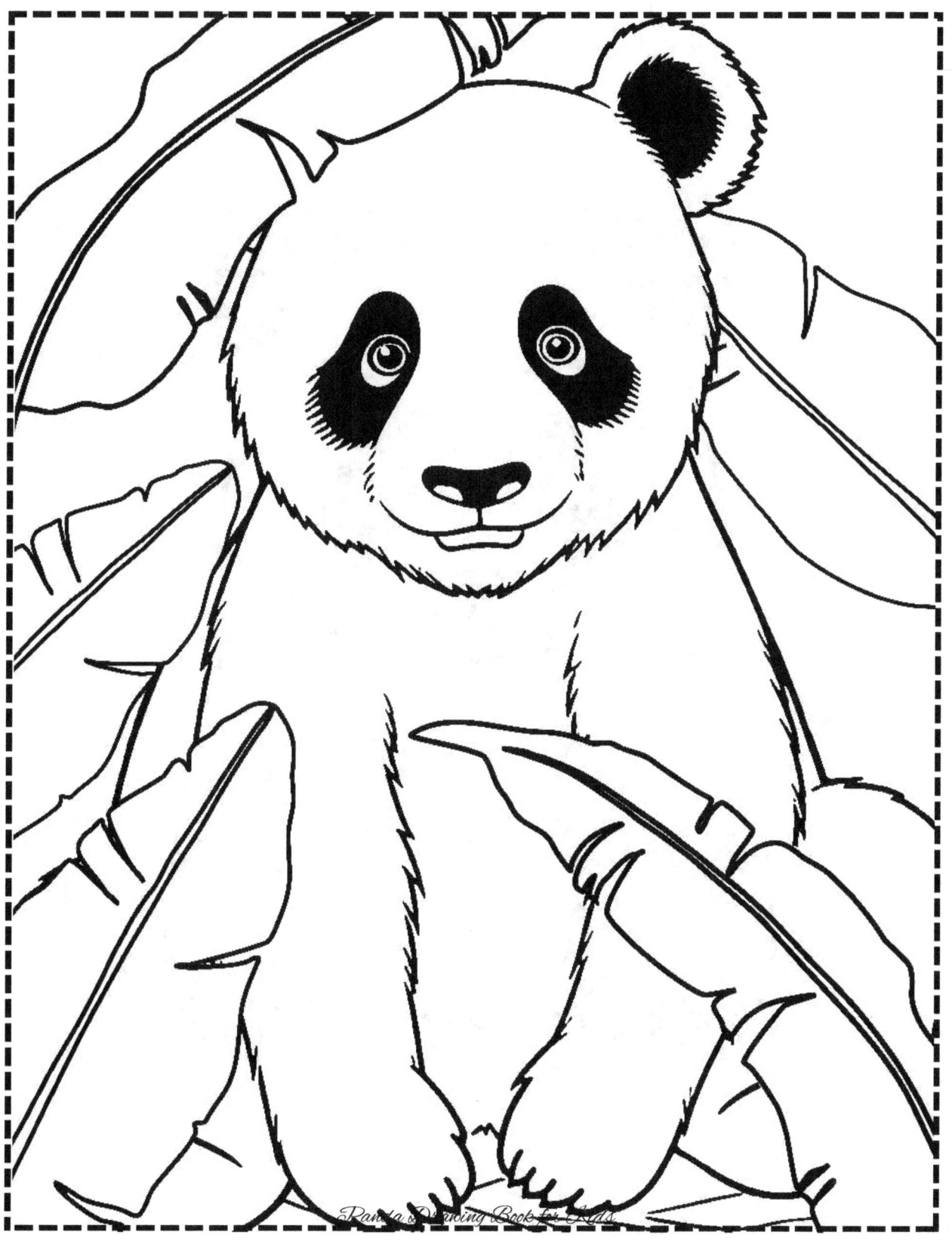

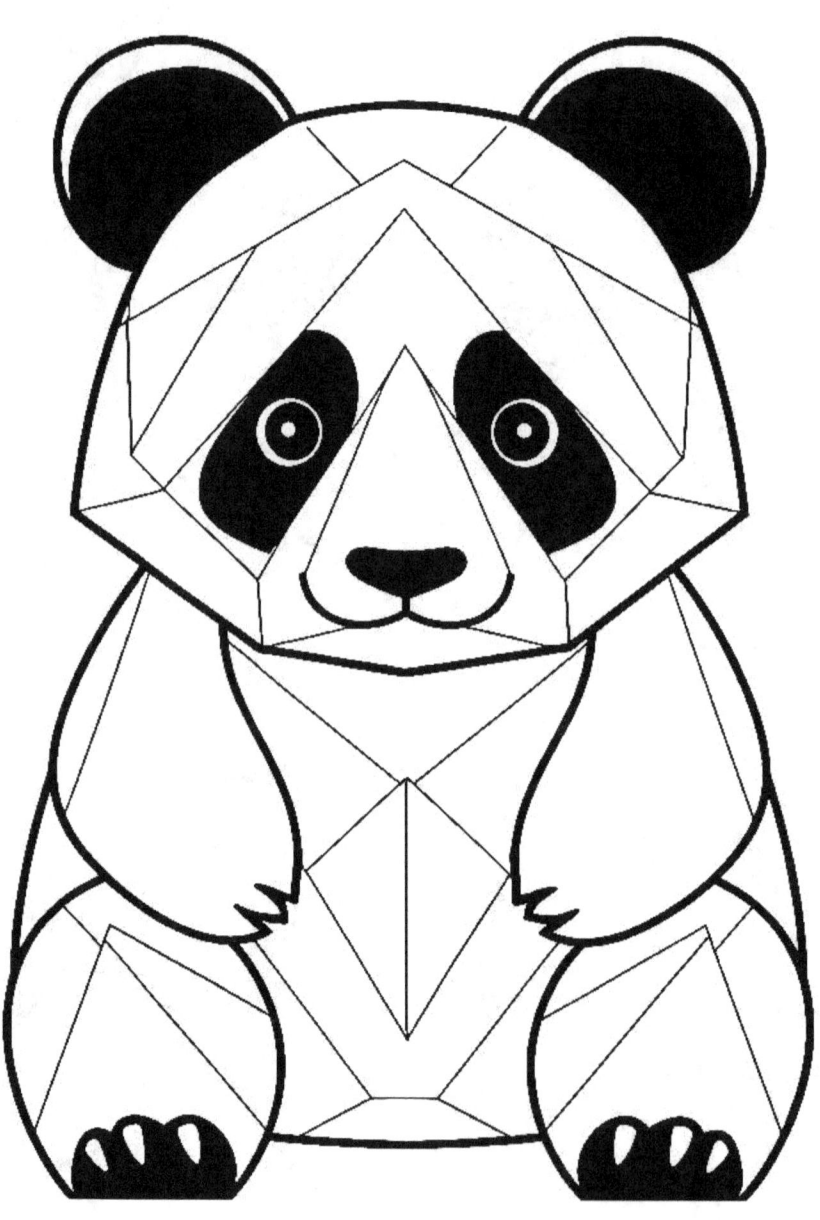

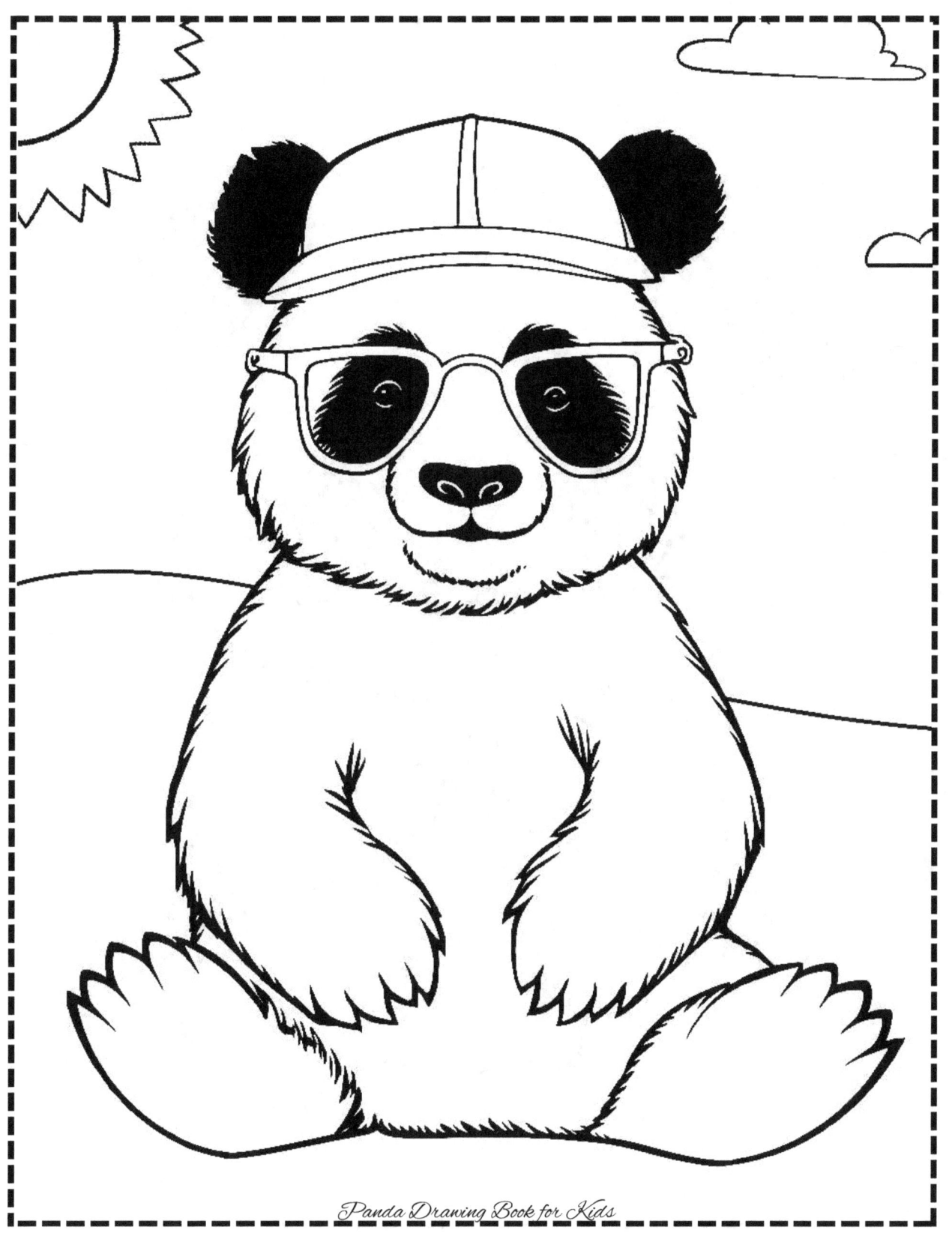

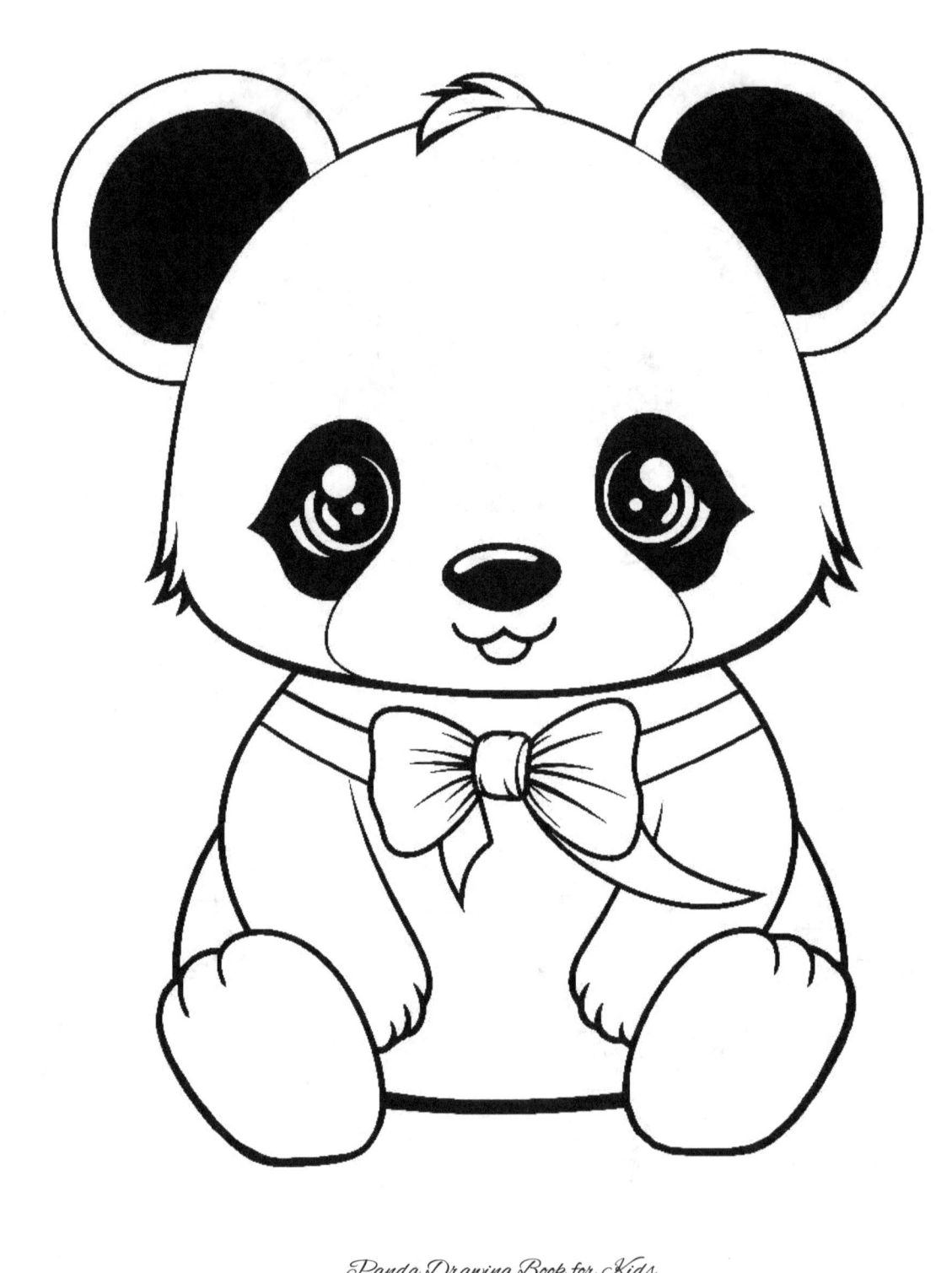

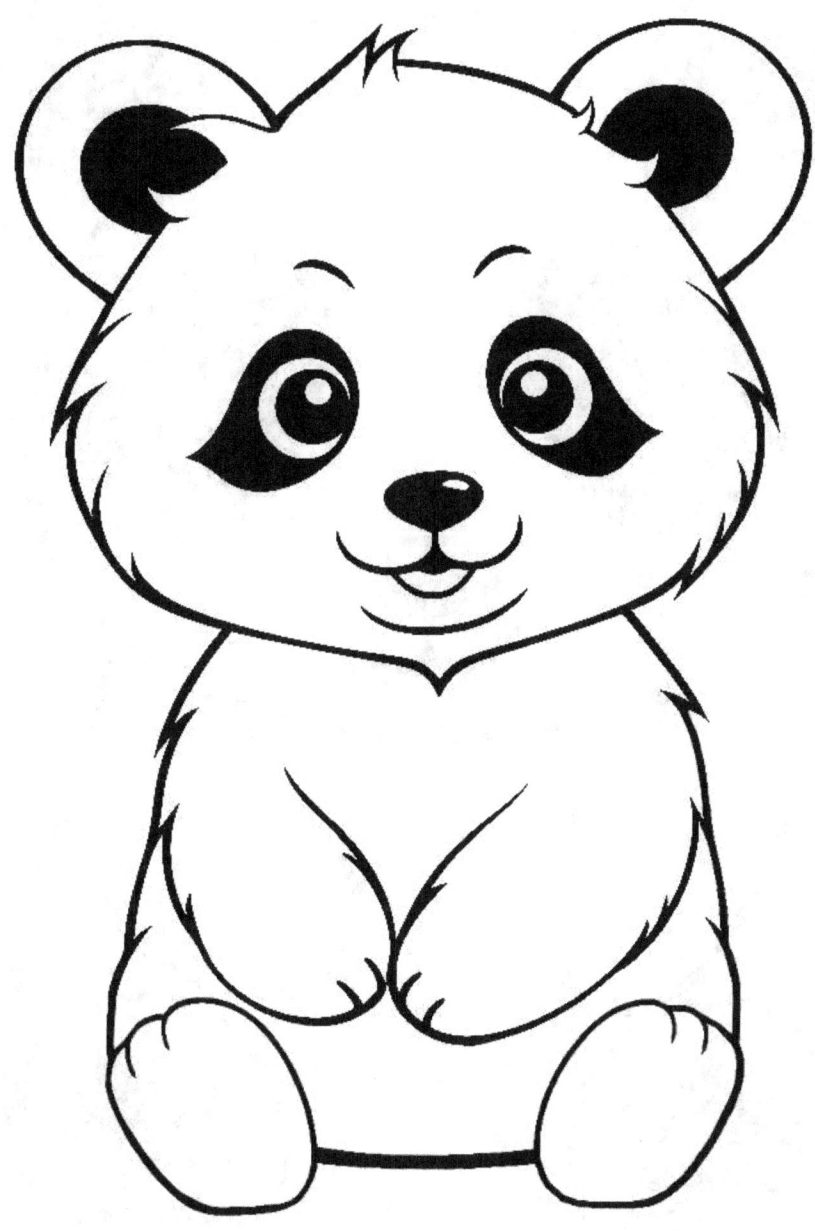

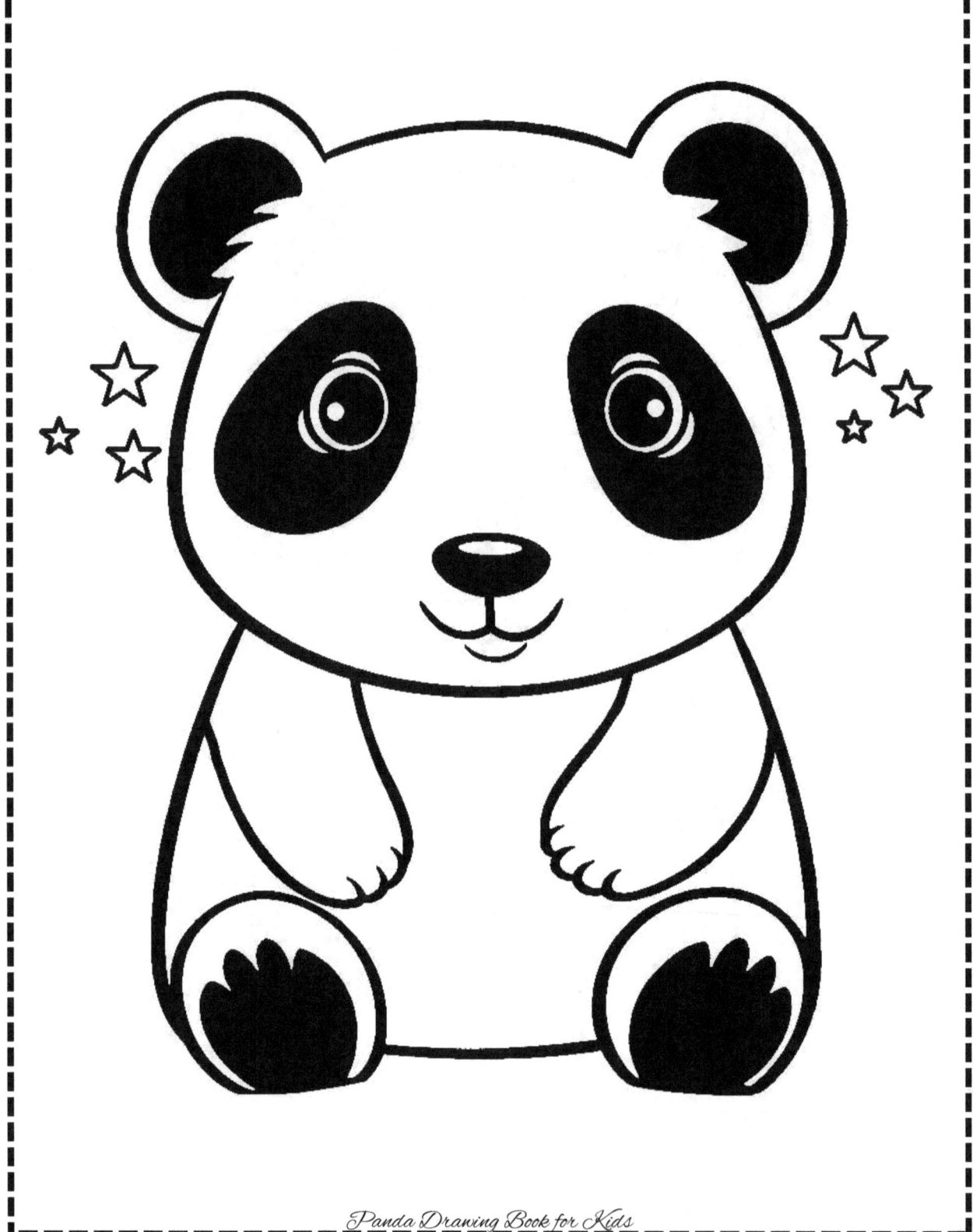

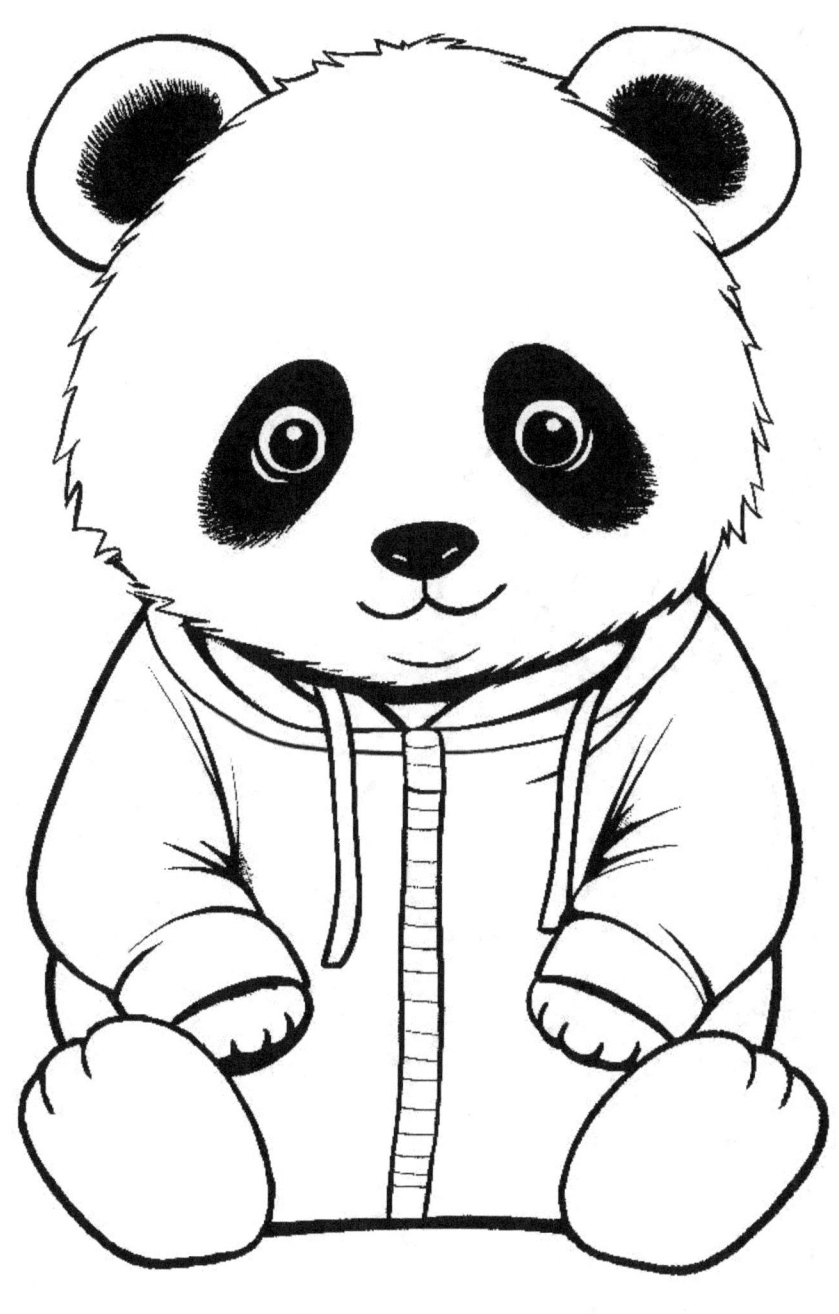

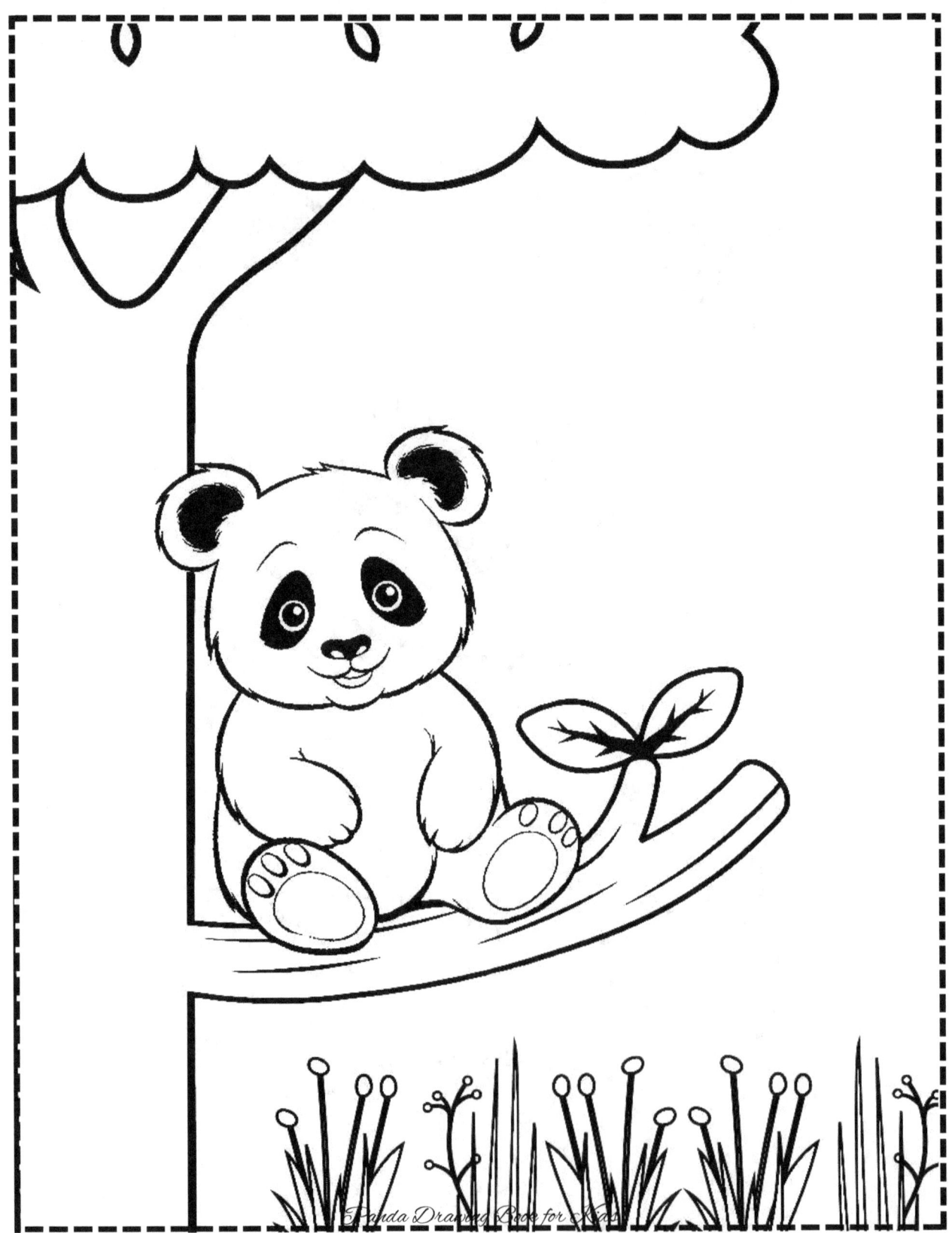

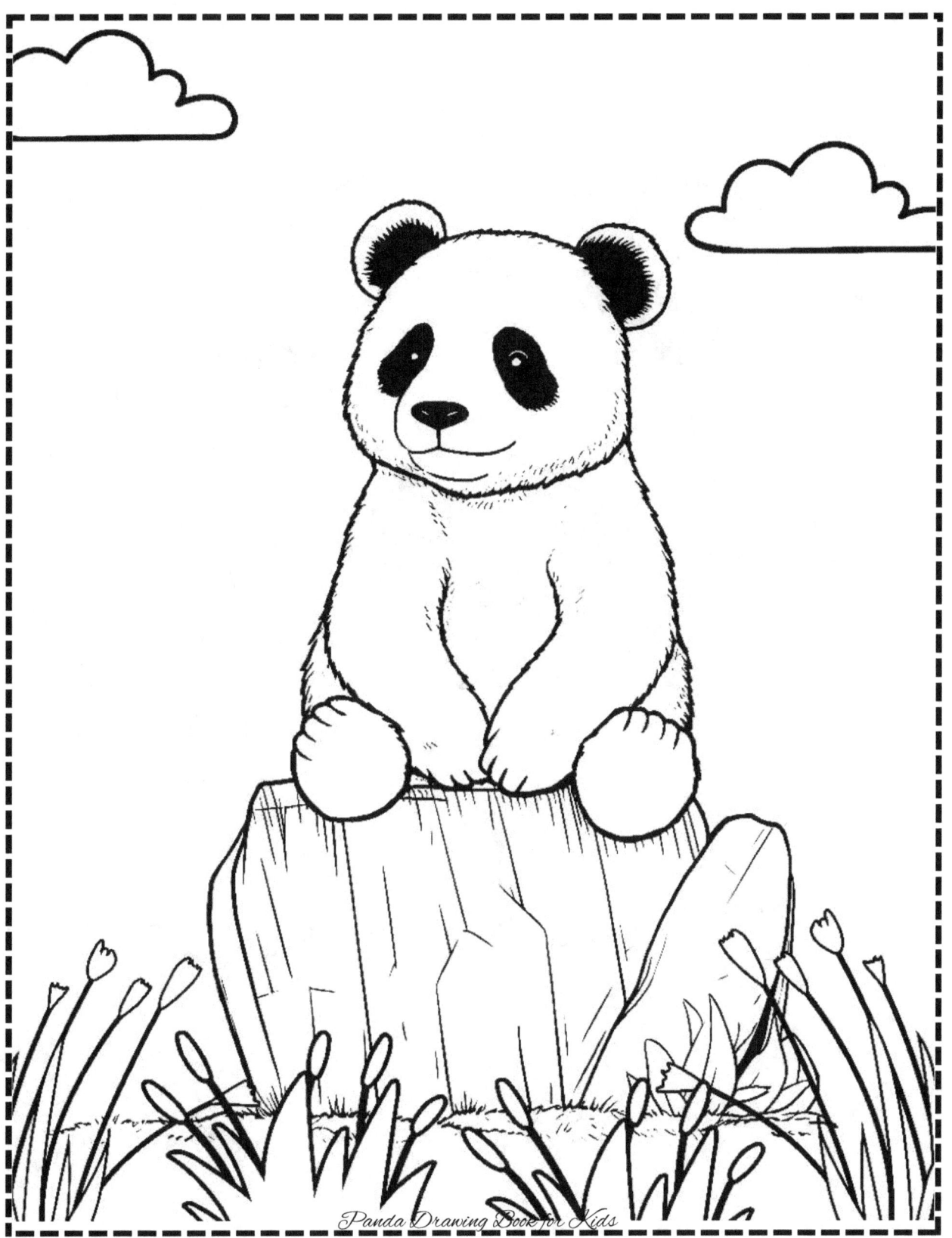

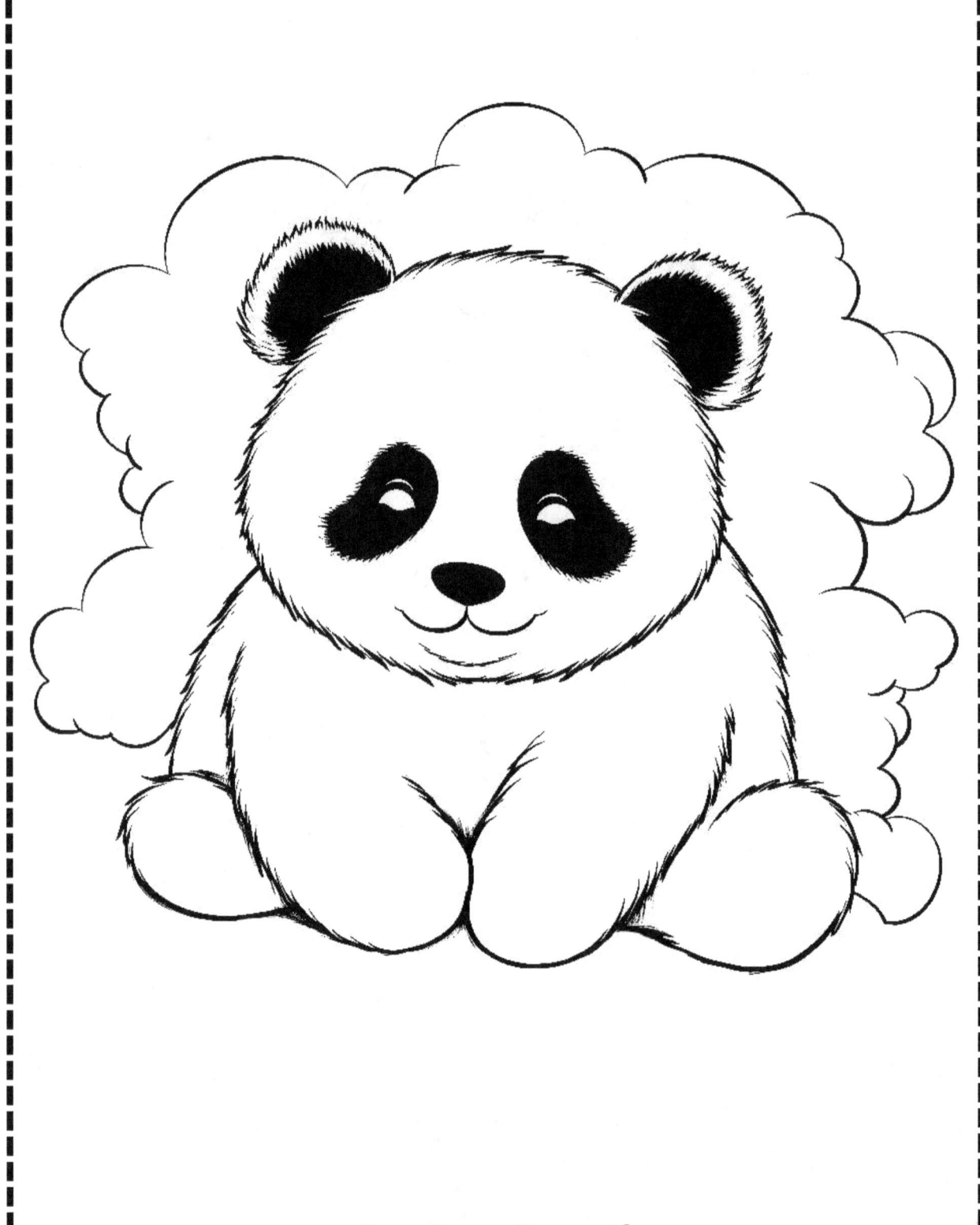

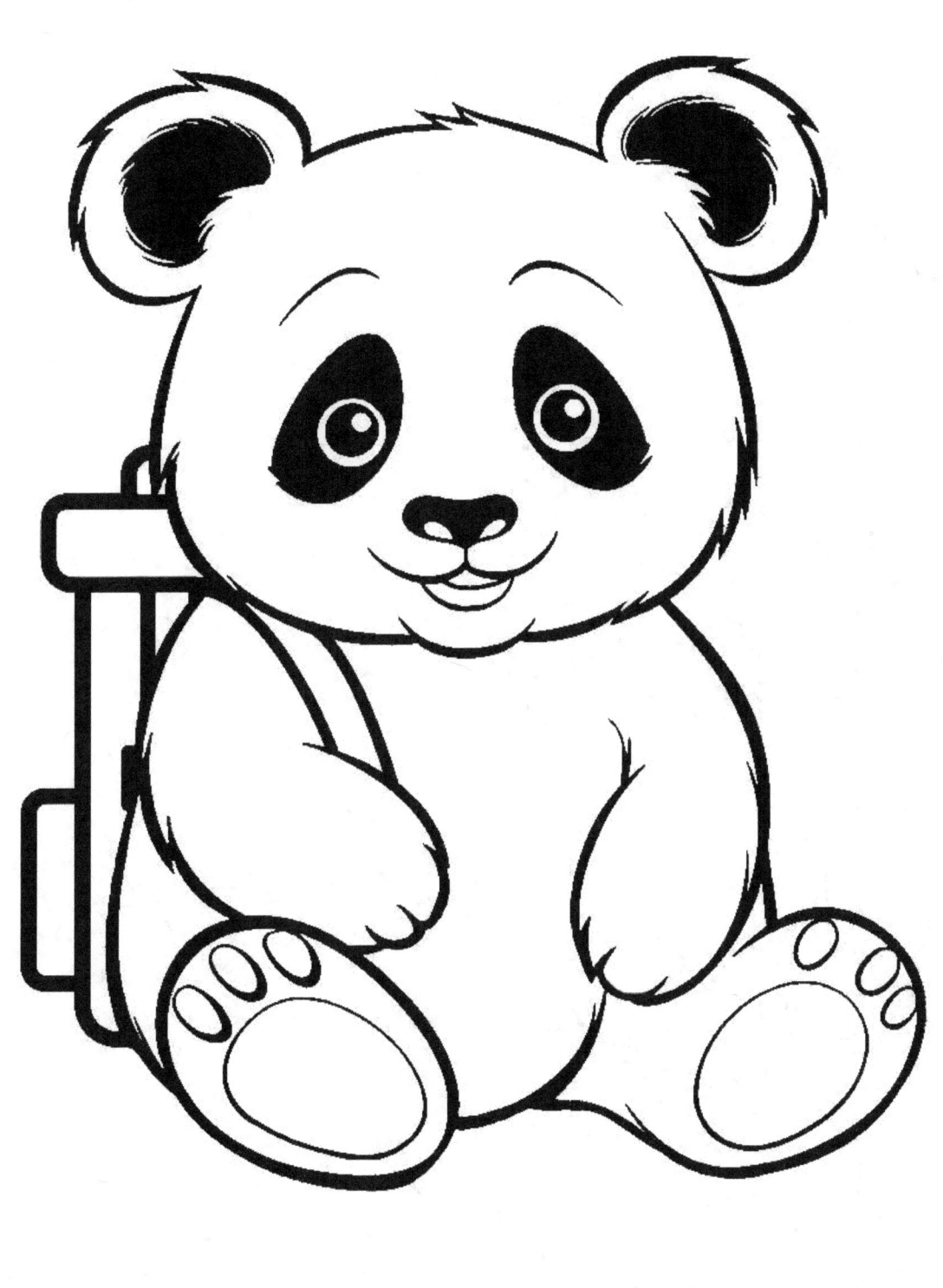

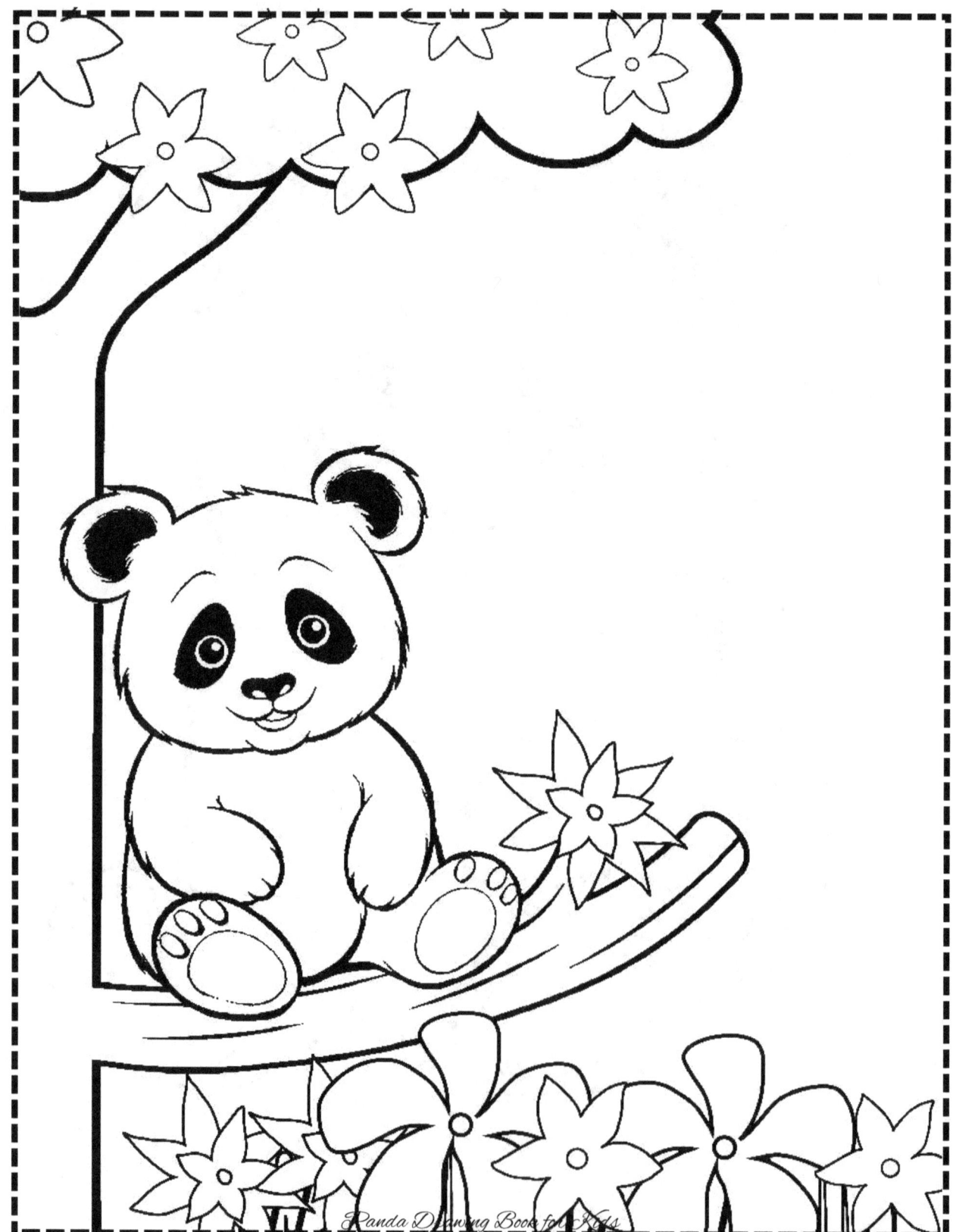

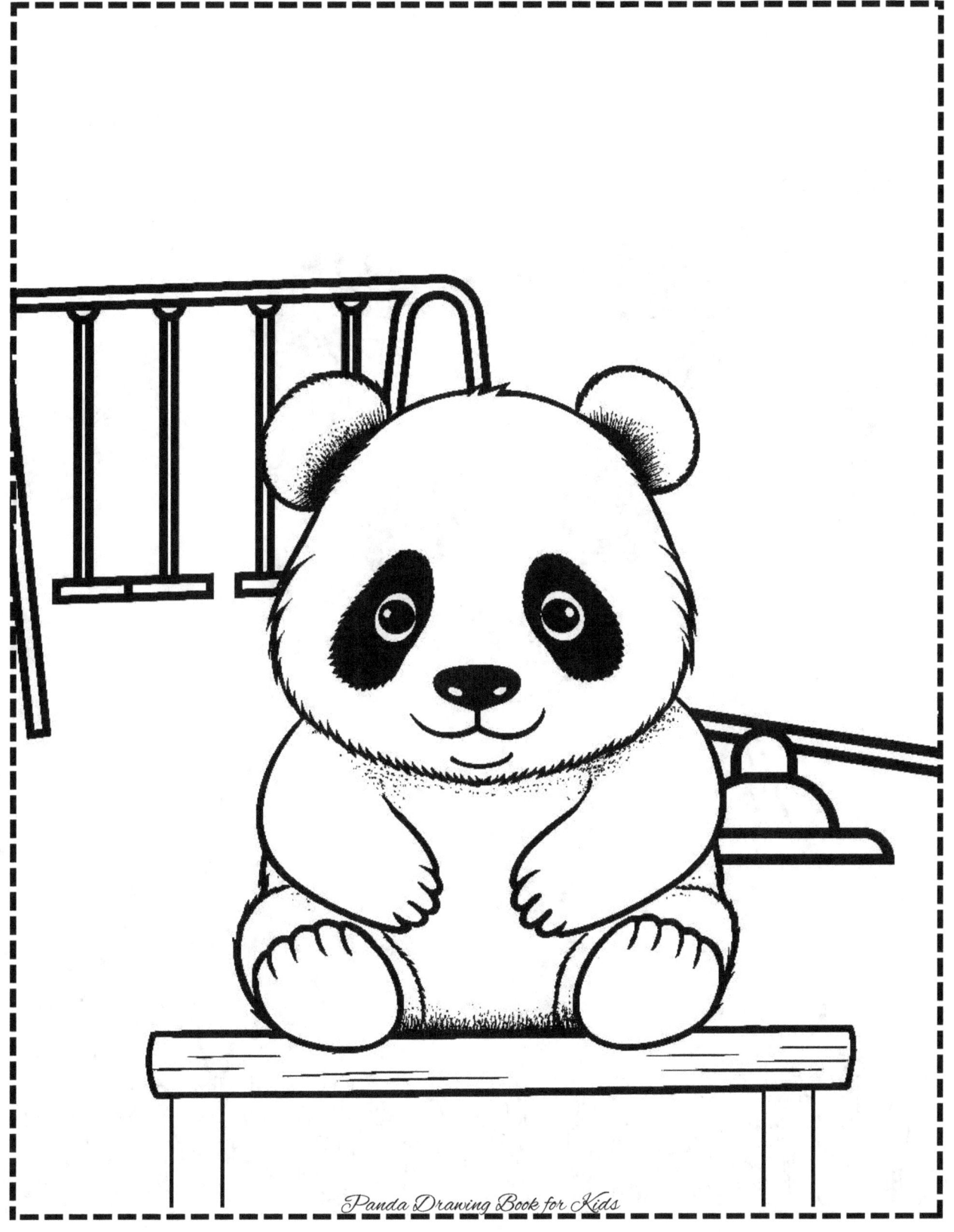

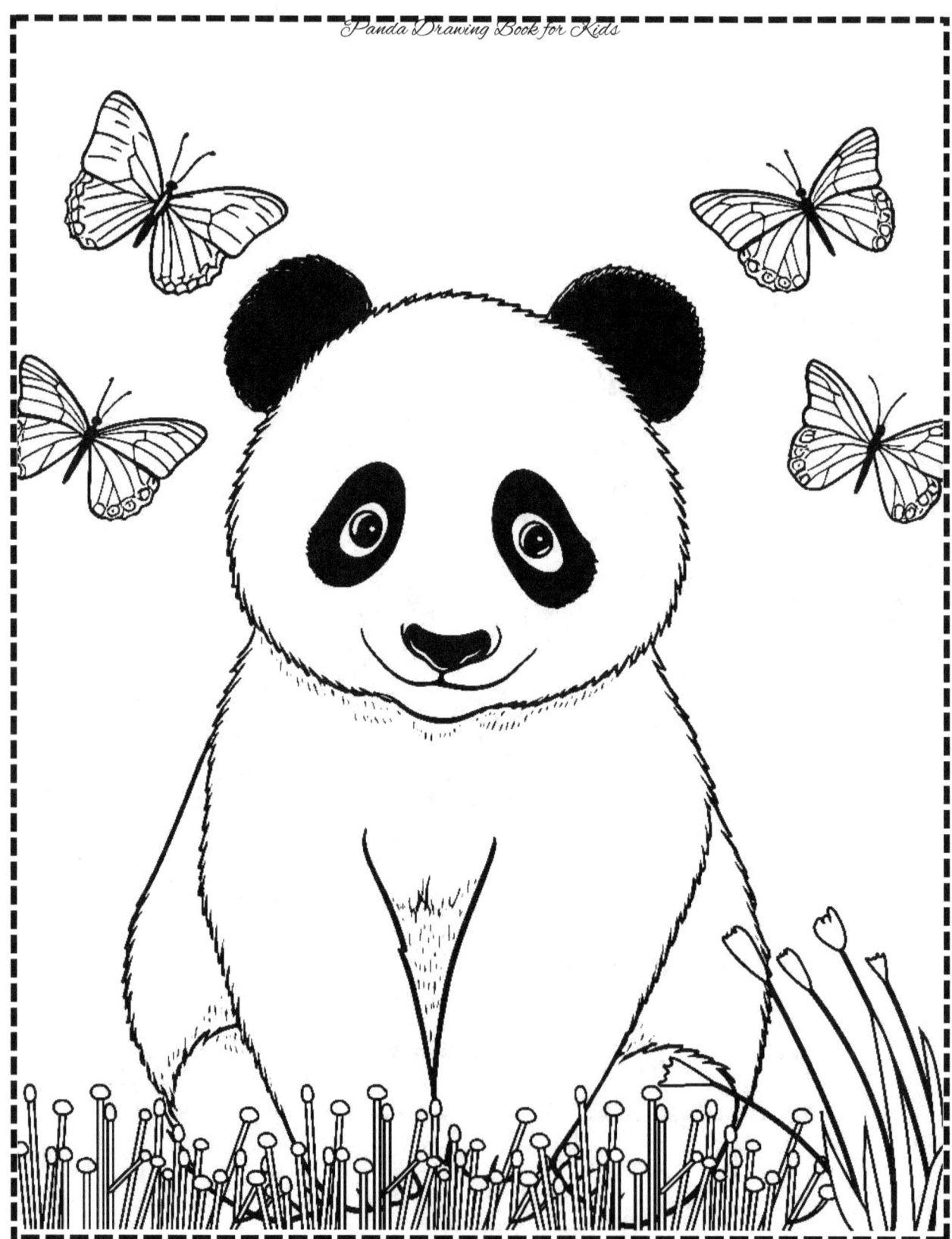

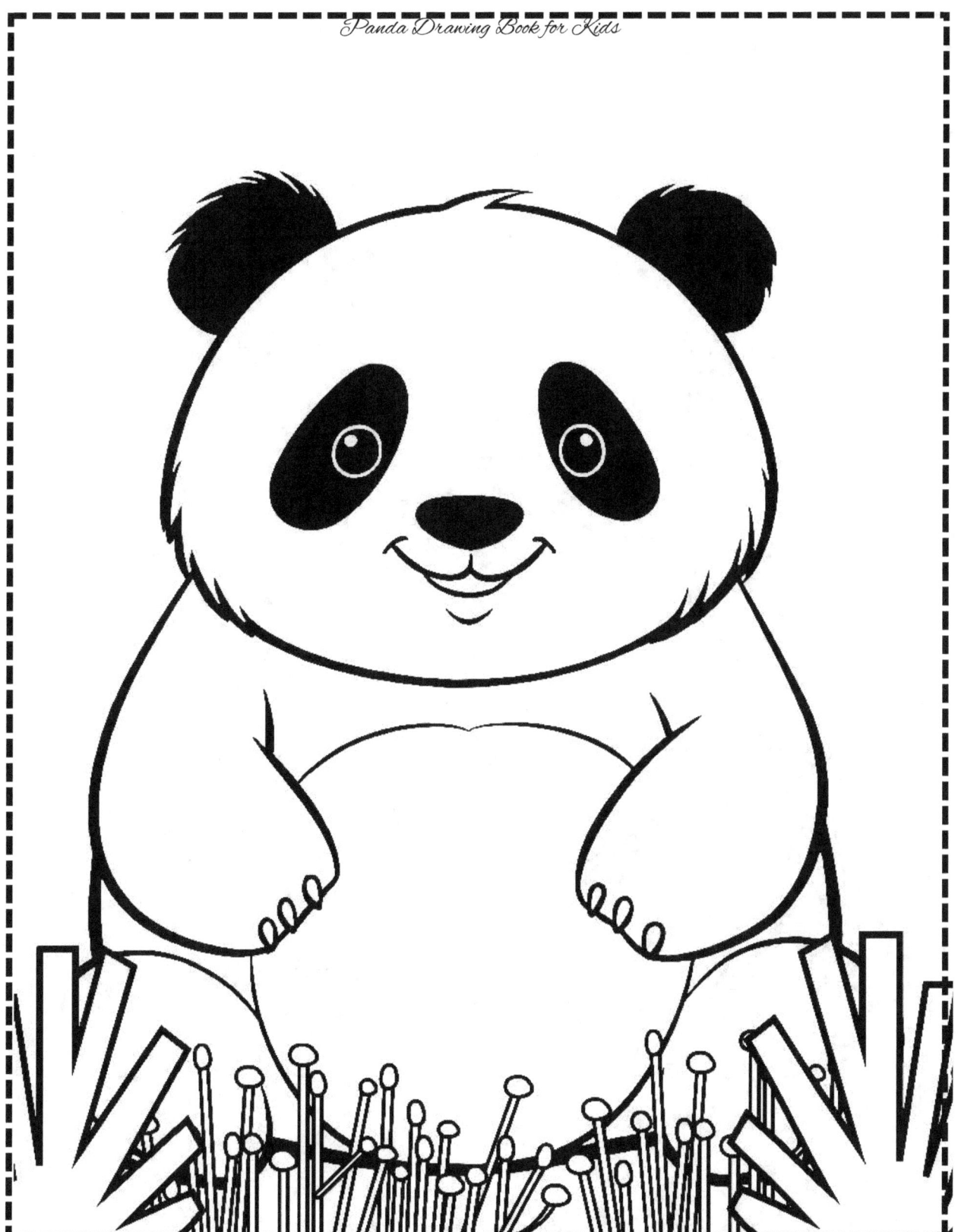

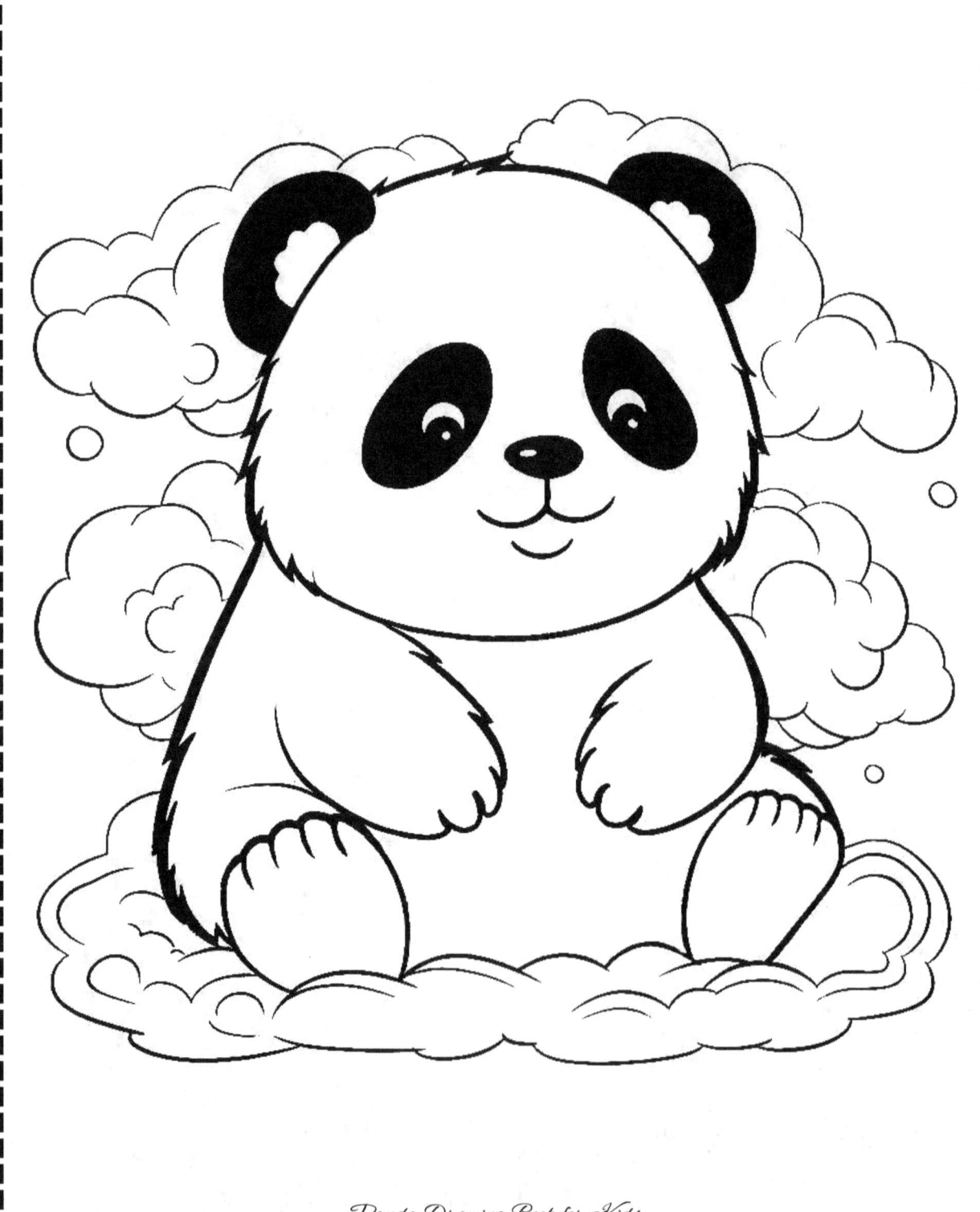

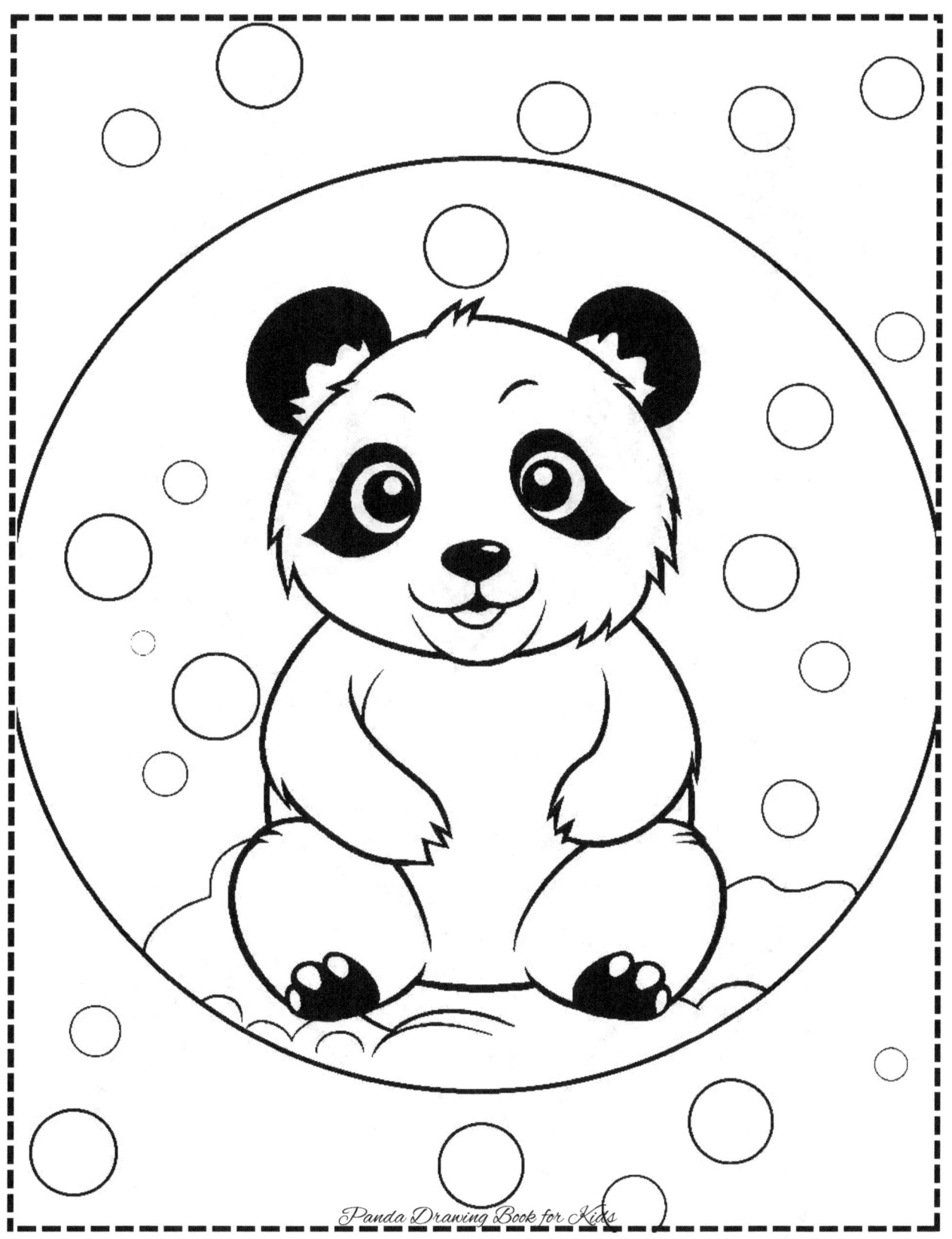

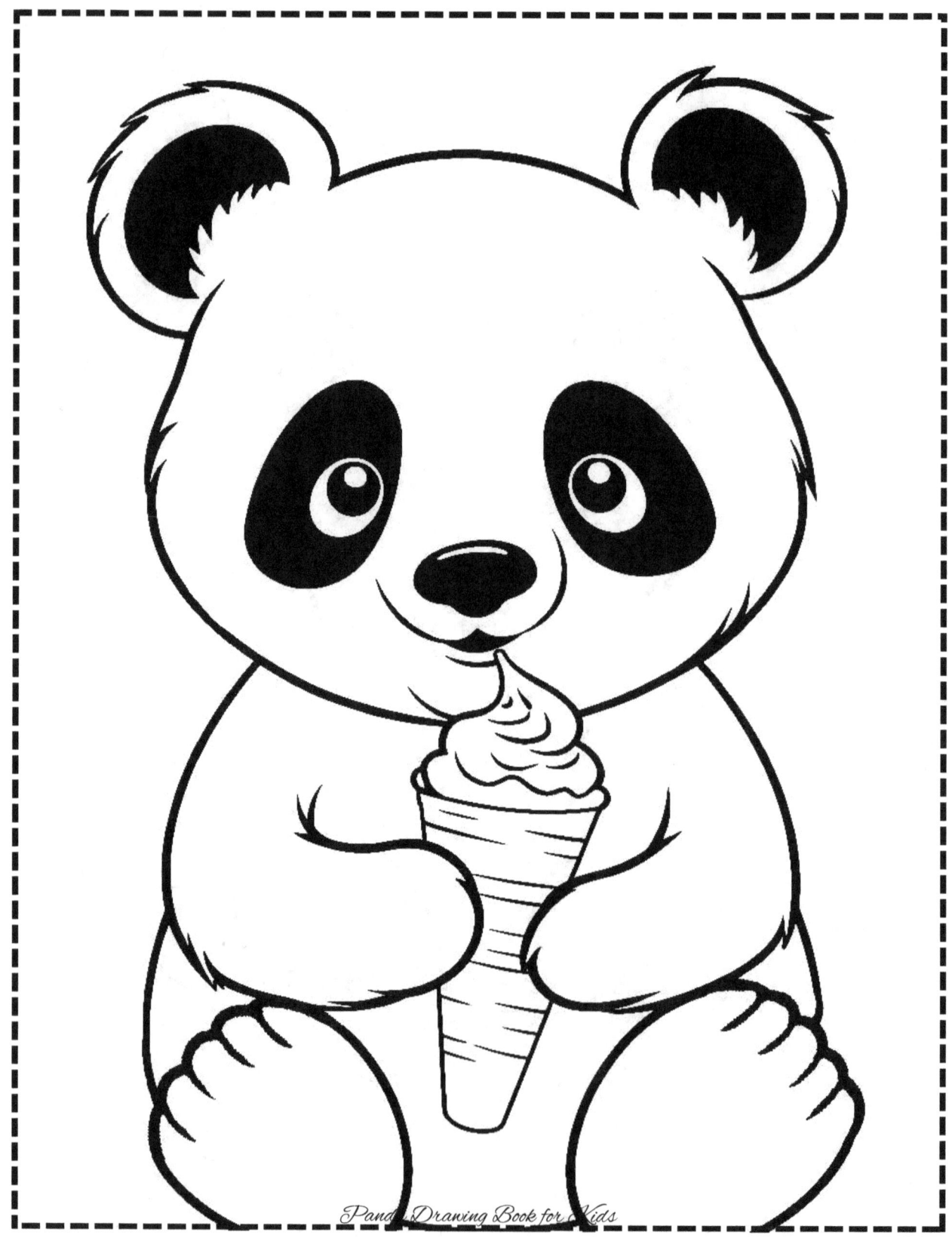

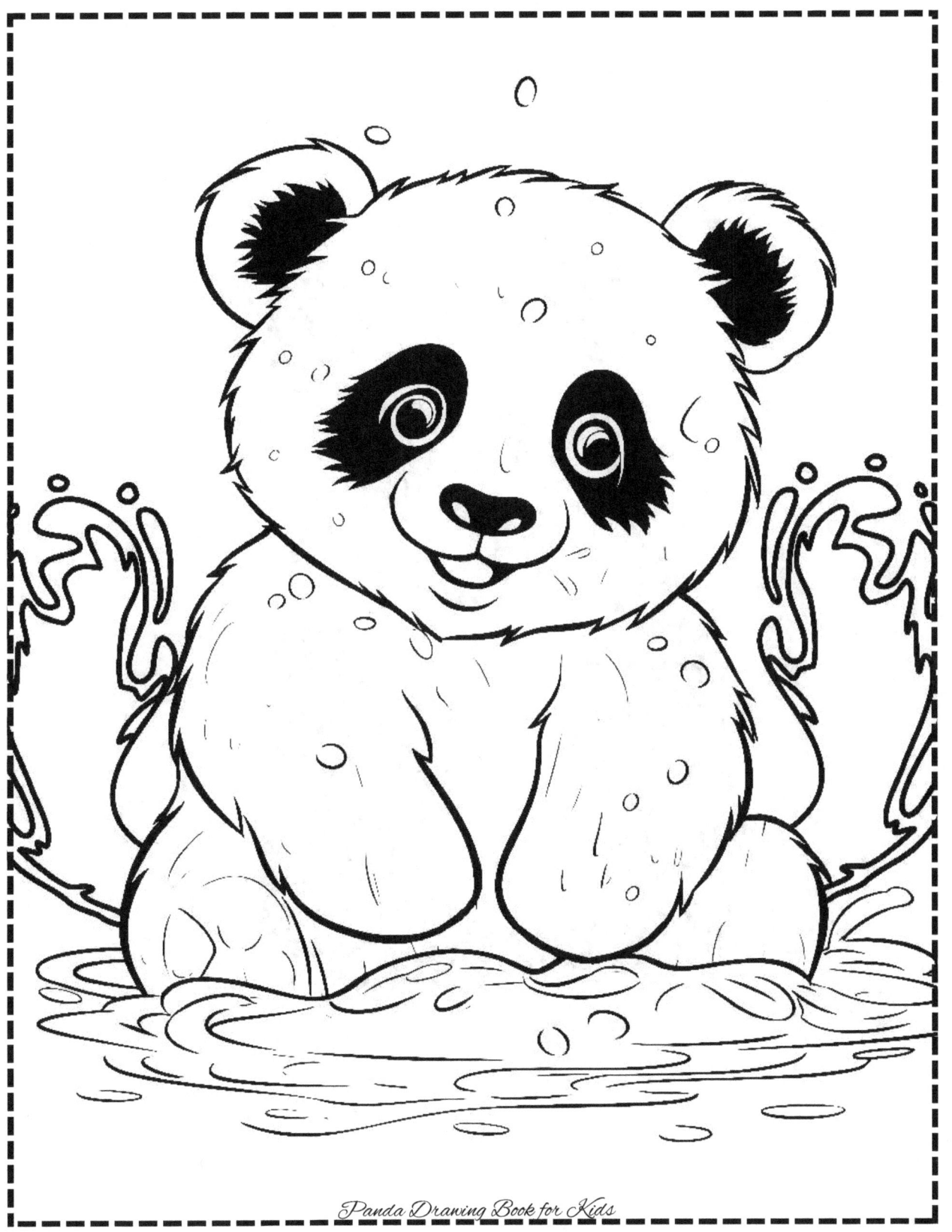

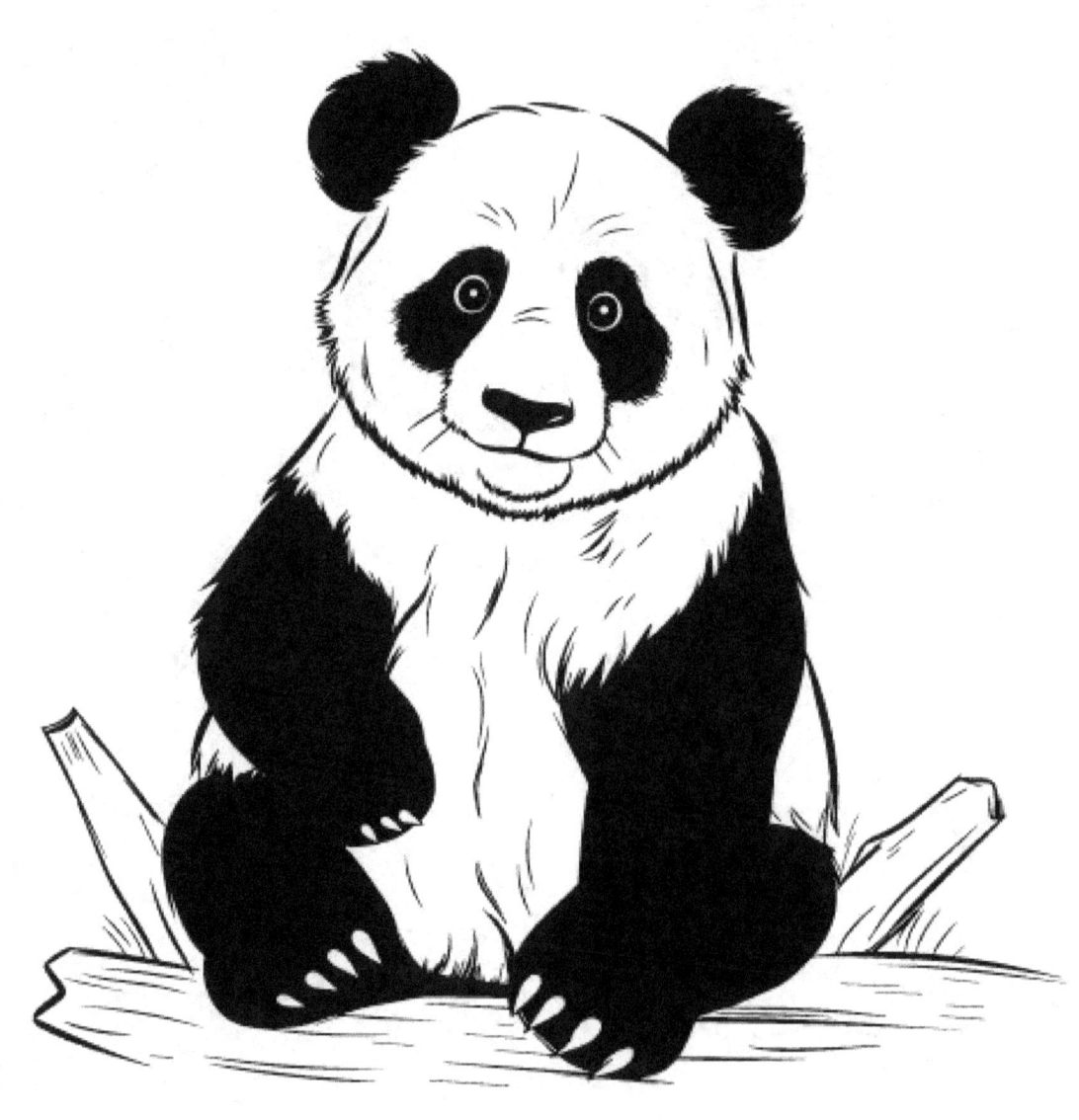

Panda Drawing Book for Kids

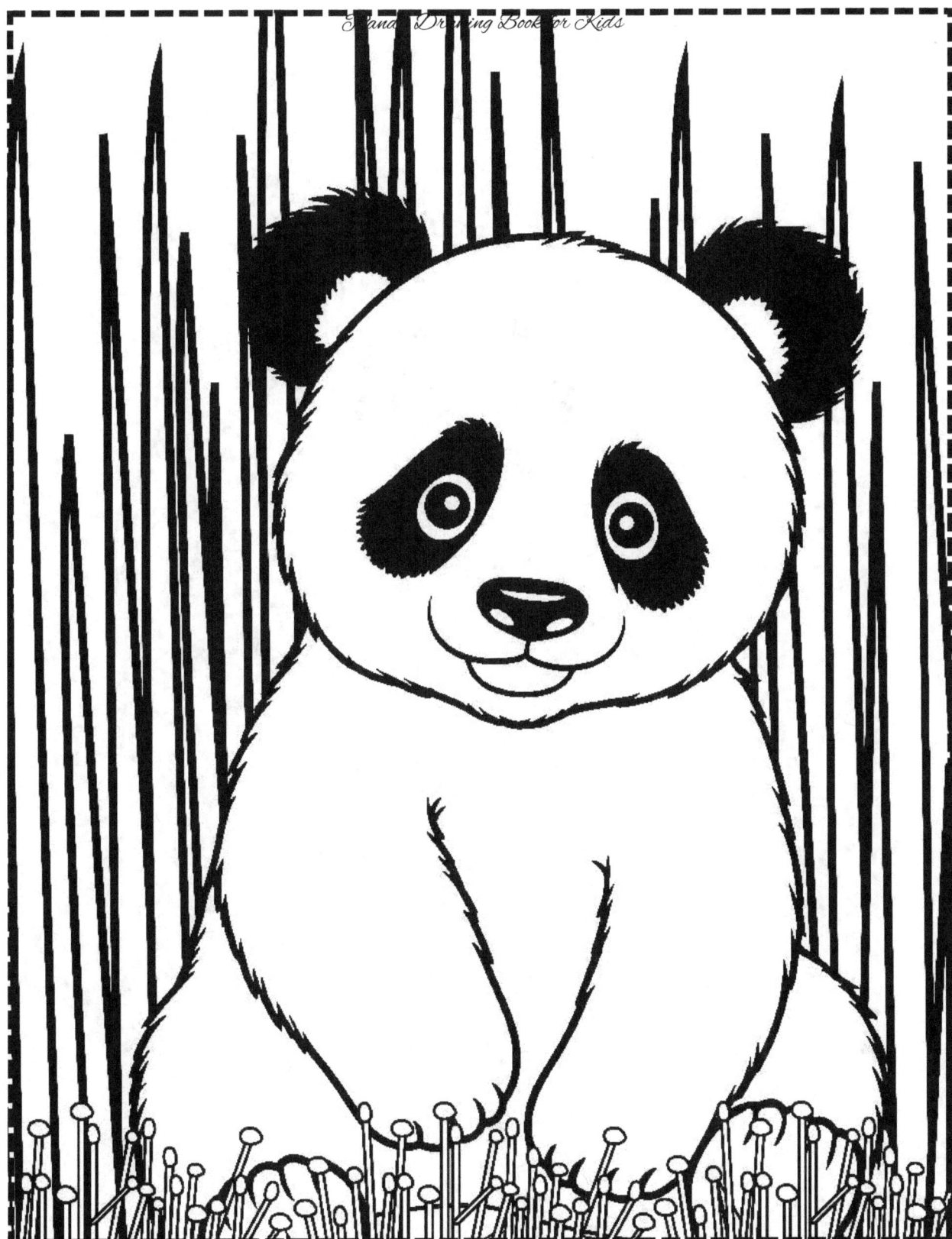

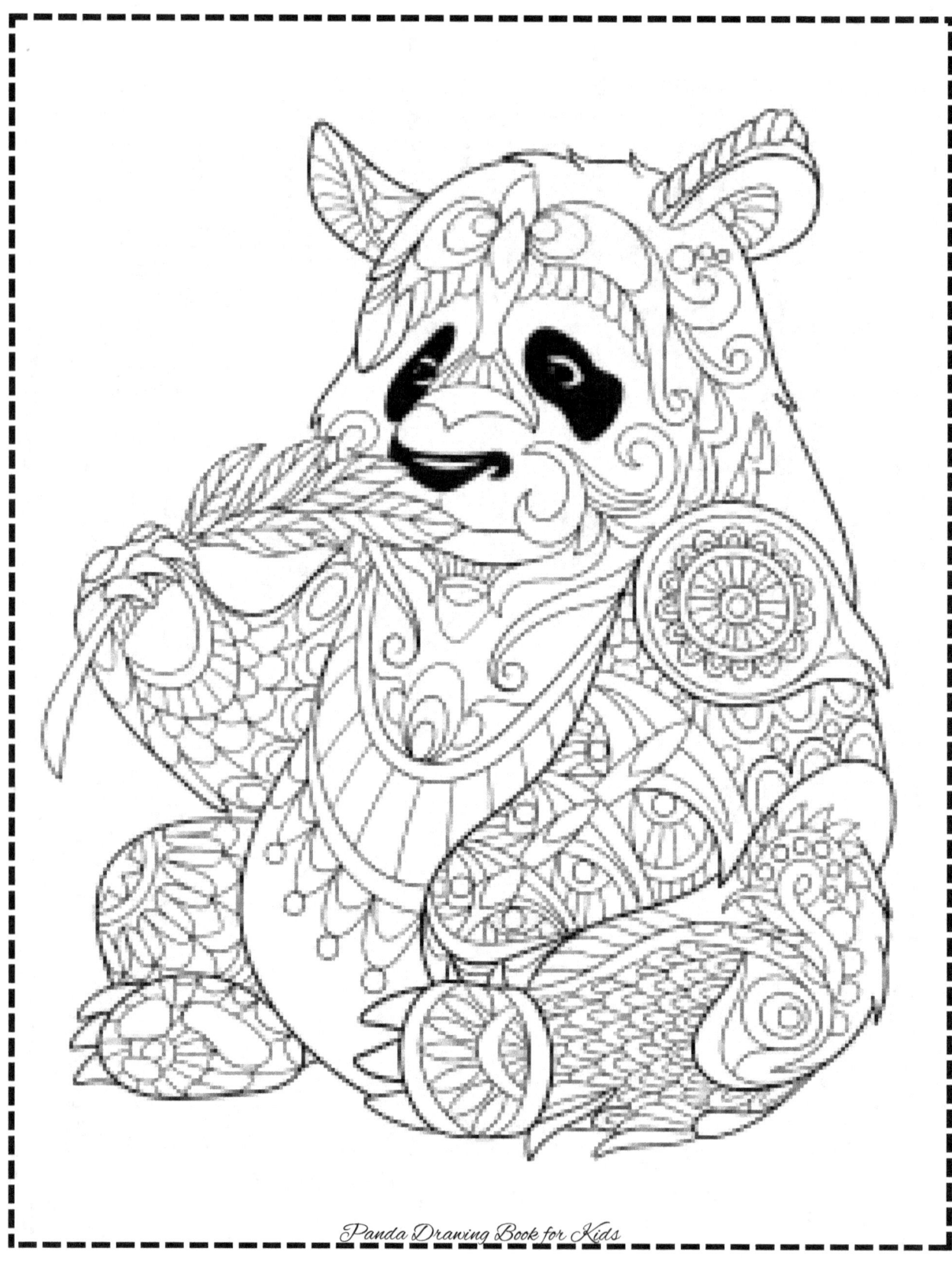

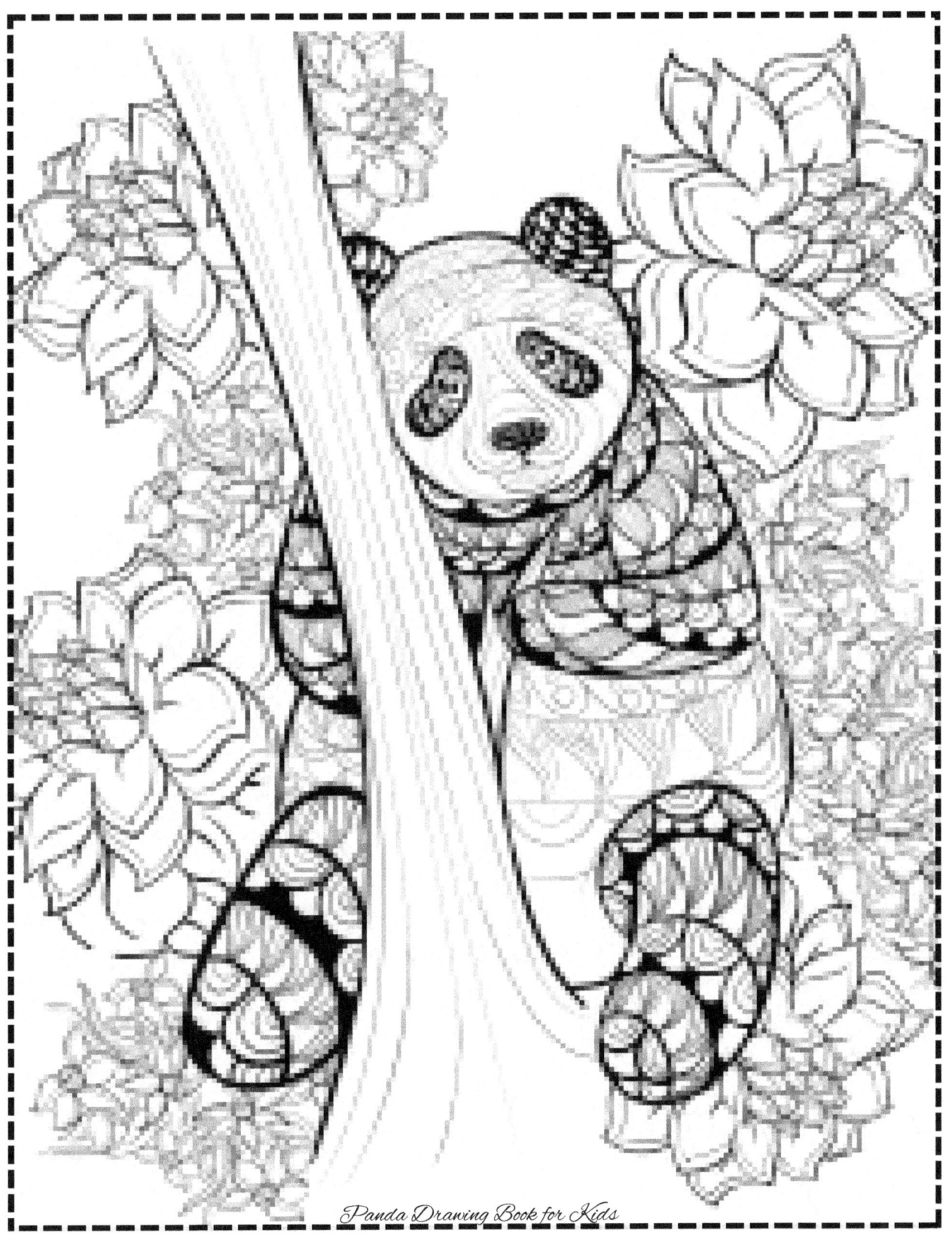

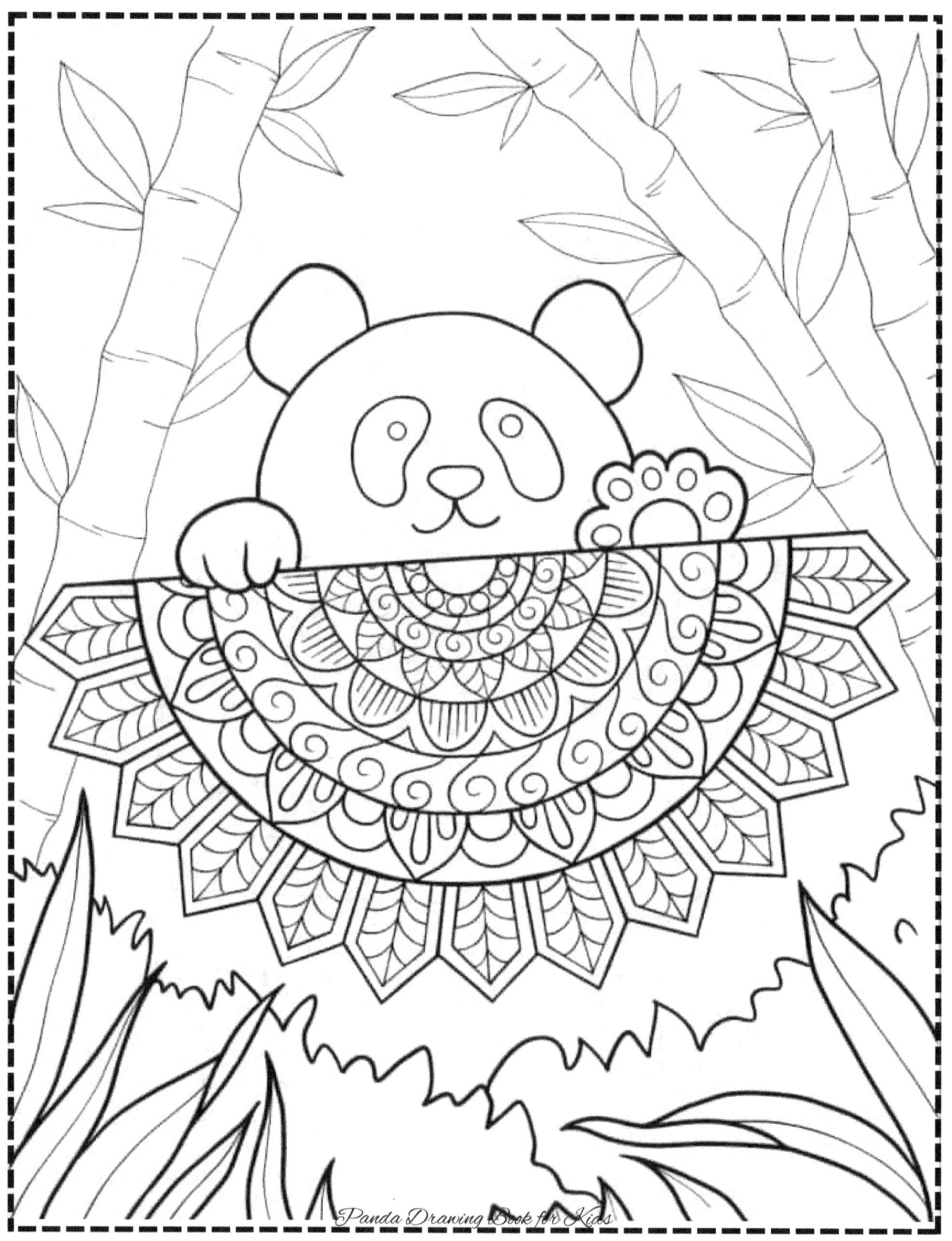

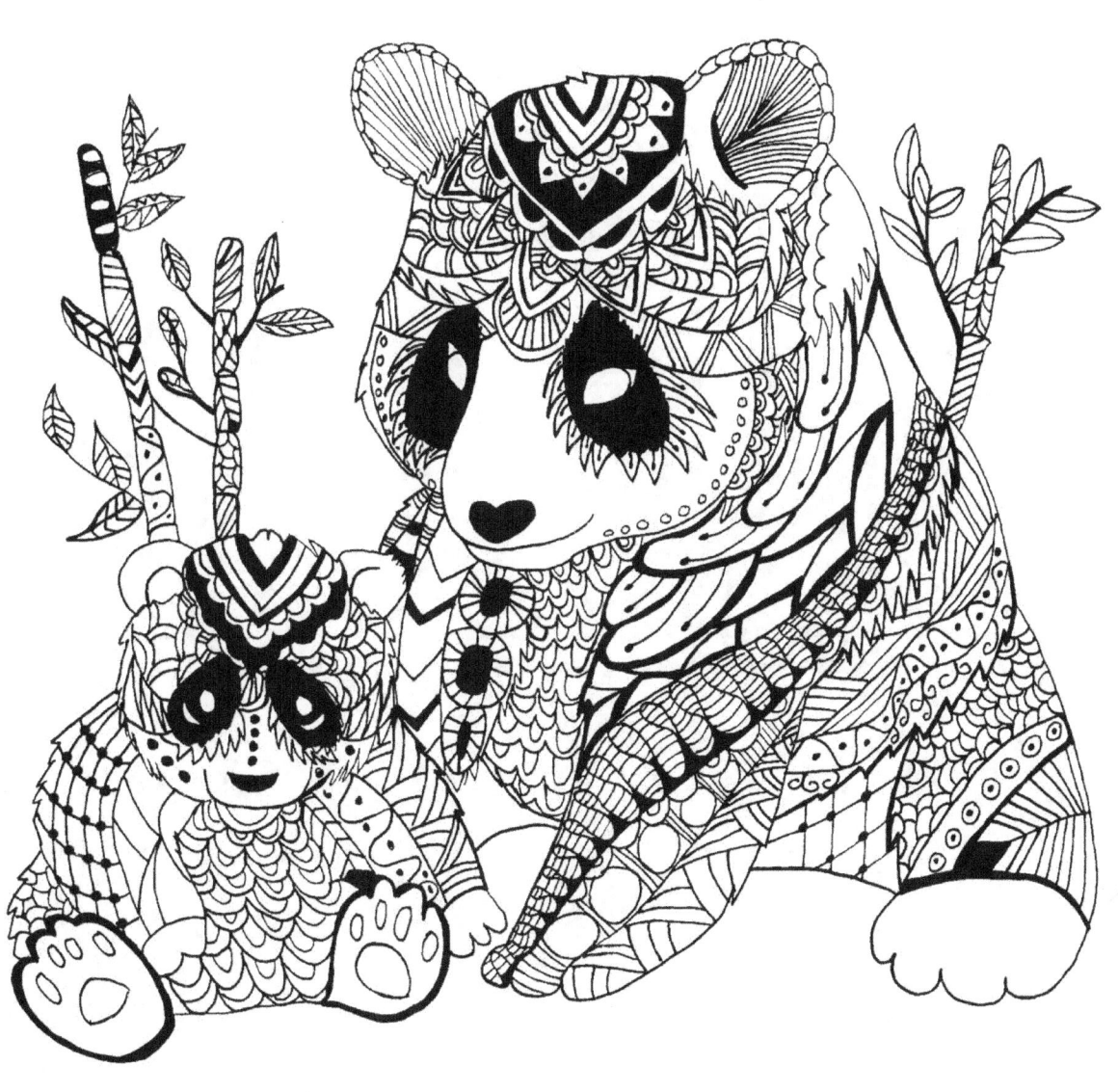